TONY HILLERMAN: A PUBLIC LIFE

PHOTO COURTESY ULF ANDERSEN, PONO PRESSE

TABLE OF CONTENTS

LIST OF ILLUSTRATIONS

INTRODUCTION

The private realm is all the rage in these troubled times. Television talk shows regale us with tales of self-inflicted wretchedness and woe. Athletes are forced to describe their feelings of exuberant joy or weepy despair for the camera, the moment they hit the big home run or fumble in the end zone. The politics of self-empowerment, despite its valuable achievements, has contributed to a massive public demonstration of self-pity and self-indulgence. Self-help books top the best-seller lists month after month and year after year. The private life, it seems, has become the public life.

And yet, not so very long ago, it was still possible to live a life characterized by *civitas*, by civic virtue — a *public* life in the best sense. In fact, there are those few rare individuals among us who continue to do so even today. One of them happens, among other things, to be an author. And remarkably, his novels have managed to muscle their way into the company of the most exalted self-help best-sellers. Odder still, despite the presence of the occasional bloodthirsty dog or flayed corpse, the books are, for the most part, distinctly free of the gruesome horror that propels Stephen King's novels to these same lists. How strange.

Tony Hillerman has written eleven Navajo mystery novels. The most recent, *Sacred Clowns*, had an initial hardcover printing of 400,000 — an astonishing number. Yet the success of these novels defies all publishing logic. Why should people wish to read about Jim Chee, Joe Leaphorn, and life on the Big Reservation? The novels lack the intricacy of plot that one might find in a John Le Carré or Len Deighton book. They lack the romance and opulence of, say, a Danielle Steel or a Judith Krantz. They have none of the made-for-TV pizzazz of John Grisham's legal labyrinths. Moreover, Hillerman's novels are about Navajos — Indians — a people who until very recently had been acknowledged in the mainstream North American psyche only as stereotypes: either noble savages or murderous killers. Why then are Tony Hillerman's novels so popular? Why have his novels succeeded in so entrancing his millions of readers?

In part, the answer lies in the character of the author, in Tony Hillerman himself. It lies in an approach to the world rarely encountered anymore — a belief that every individual is intimately connected to his or her environment in innumerable ways, that such links are essentially moral, and that it is the responsibility of each individual to ensure that these links, which are the common ground of the community — are in fact nothing less than the *communitas* itself — remain healthy and ordered. In the Navajo world, these links run between the individual and the natural world, as well as between the individual and the community. And while most inhabitants of North America have long since abandoned any genuine connection to the earth, deep in the heart of all commuting, computer-operating, MTV-watching members of our society lies a desire to reattach those severed connections to both the human community and the natural world. Tony Hillerman's novels offer a glimpse of what that might mean. And his life, perhaps even more so than his books, does the same.

Long before becoming a best-selling author, Tony Hillerman had committed himself to these ideals. Long before his success as a writer of fiction, he distinguished himself as a journalist, an educator, and a community leader. And so, while the publishing industry may see the success of Hillerman's novels as an anomaly, in the context of Hillerman's lifelong commitment to the people and places that have surrounded him, it is not. Hillerman's novels are simply an enormous expansion of that relationship, one characterized for the past fifty years by mutual respect and support.

★　★　★　★

When I set out to write this brief biography, my aim was to discover the man behind the novels, the enigmatic figure known to the many who love his work primarily through a brief dust-jacket blurb and a postage stamp–sized black-and-white photo above it. The photo most commonly used is intriguing. In it, we see *Hillerman*, as he is known to his readers, standing before some sort of log cabin — a hogan perhaps. He appears old and wizened, yet youthful and firm at the same time. His eyes stare at the camera with a gaze that gives away nothing. His hair is confusing — it appears to be braided, or in some other way unusually coiffed. And those high cheekbones — one inevitably wonders, Is Hillerman a Navajo? Does he share some other native ancestry? Or is he a white man with a deep understanding of Navajo culture? If so, where did that understanding come from? Who is this outsider who has so captured the inner qualities of a people, a land, a way of life?

The answers to these questions lie ahead. But so does a great deal more. For in researching the life of Tony Hillerman, I discovered that he has lived an enormous amount of it both in the public eye and in public service. Tony Hillerman has been tremendously responsive over the years to the demands and requests placed upon him by neighbours, friends, students, and countless strangers. Yet when I approached him concerning this biography, he was resolute in his refusal to be interviewed. And the more I learned about the many contributions he had already made, the more I felt uncomfortable intruding upon the well-earned privacy of a man in his seventies.

Thus, I realized that I had been afforded an unusual opportunity — rather than invading Tony Hillerman's privacy, rather than splashing his most intimate memories and activities across the page like a literary Geraldo, I could recount the public life of a man respected by all who know him. And this I have set out to do. Precisely because Tony Hillerman has been so responsive to others — granting countless interviews, writing endless letters — the wealth of material offering insight into his thoughts and experiences is staggering. And it has all been placed in the public domain by Hillerman himself. In the scores of interviews he has given, there is a clear division between the public and the private. Hillerman speaks of his public actions with humour and candour, yet he offers virtually nothing in the way of insight into his family life as the father of six children, five of whom were adopted. I have chosen to respect that division, and so there will be little in the way of personal drama. What there will be in abundance, however, throughout these pages, is the drama of a man with an exceptional sensitivity and courage, deeply committed to his community. A man who, though modest, has forever changed the world he lives in.

I

On April 2, 1969, a letter arrived on Joan Kahn's desk asking her to settle a dispute. The dispute was about a manuscript, a suspense novel to be titled either "Enemy Way" or "Monster-slayer." Both the letter and the manuscript were written by a journalist in Albuquerque, New Mexico, named Tony Hillerman, who explained that while he felt certain that the Indian ritual elements of his novel were essential to the mood and plot, his agent, Ann Elmo, felt they ought to be cut. Could he please submit the novel for Joan Kahn's expert editorial assessment?

This frank yet somewhat sly letter might easily have been tossed in the trash alongside countless other publishing might-have-beens. As the editor of the Harper Novel of Suspense Series, Joan Kahn received an endless stream of unsolicited manuscripts and letters from unheralded authors convinced they had written the next *Red Harvest* or *Maltese Falcon*. Yet this particular letter received an almost instant reply, saying yes, by all means, send it along. So on April 10, Tony Hillerman airmailed his first novel to Harper and Row Publishers in New York City.

Coincidentally, Hillerman was scheduled to be in New York only ten days later, attending a gathering of journalism department chairs. Though he recognized the unlikeliness of Joan Kahn having anything to tell him so soon, he nonetheless called her shortly after he arrived. To his amazement, she told him Harper and Row would publish the book. Of course it would need a new ending, and a new title, and rather than playing down the Indian elements, he'd have to beef them up — but still, it was good.

Although the money Hillerman received for this first novel was modest ($3,500), he felt tremendous vindication at being published by a major publisher. Not because he had proven his agent wrong, but because in 1970 at the age of forty-four, with more than two decades of professional writing behind him, he had finally managed to simply "tell a story," to abandon the rigorous demands of journalism for the freewheeling world of the imagination, and to do so in a way that pleased others.

For the past seven years, ever since giving up his position as executive editor of the Santa Fe *New Mexican* and returning to university to study English literature, Hillerman had looked forward to writing fiction. With a simple word of approval from Joan Kahn, the sacrifices, the risks — after all, he had chosen, with his wife Marie's encouragement, to leave a successful career at the age of thirty-seven and to return to school despite having six children to support — all these uncertainties were suddenly conquered and a major ambition realized.

Now, finally, Tony Hillerman would be able to forget all that Navajo stuff and get on to writing the book he really wanted to write!

★   ★   ★   ★

When *The Blessing Way*, as that first novel was eventually titled, was published in 1970, Tony Hillerman began what was to be his third career. Not surprisingly, given the success he has achieved as an author, Hillerman had been no slouch in his first two careers either. In fact, his successes in the worlds of journalism, academia, and literature signal a triple triumph almost unheard of among writers. And yet, remarkably, Hillerman as a young man had never had any intention of being a writer. The suggestion was to come to him as a result of a highly circuitous chain of events, one that began, not so unusually for men of his generation, at Pearl Harbour, when the Japanese attack prompted the United States to enter World War II.

In early 1943 Tony Hillerman was a seventeen-year-old freshman at Oklahoma State University. The campus at Stillwater was about one hundred miles north of the hamlet of Sacred Heart, where Hillerman had spent his entire life. His older brother Barney had enlisted in the army and was already overseas. Tony, like most American boys his age, couldn't wait to join him. Hillerman spent hours reading newspaper reports and watching newsreels. He collected information on troop movements like they were batting averages and division standings.

I was . . . scared to death the War would end before I could get in it. I was a war lover. It wasn't just good and bad, a fight against evil. I was just plain fascinated by war. When I went into the infantry I could name every Italian tank, armament, which kind of grenades they issued German paratroopers, and the operating range of a Fiat. I was crazy about that sort of stuff. I knew exactly how many destroyers the German navy had. (*Talking Mysteries* 115–16)

Enrolled in Chemistry, Hillerman had struggled through his first semester with low marks. By springtime even passing grades were becoming a challenge. So, determined to be a part of history, Hillerman left school, convinced his mother to sell the family farm, and upon turning eighteen embarked on the greatest adventure of his young life.

Yet, to his surprise, because he had scored so highly on his entrance exams, he was almost immediately returned to Stillwater for training in an elite group called the Army Specialized Training Corps. This lasted just a few weeks, however, as the army brass soon decided that they had more pressing need of these fresh young bodies elsewhere, and Hillerman found himself thrust into the mainstream of the United States Army, as a rifleman in the 103rd Division.

Hillerman landed in France on D-Day and spent the next eight months fighting his way through southern France. His company, the 410th Infantry, suffered enormous losses as they battled across the Rhone River Valley and Vosges Mountains. By the time Hillerman eventually returned to America, only eight members of the original regiment of two hundred were left alive. One evening in Alsace, in February 1945, Hillerman nearly joined those lost in action.

We were on one of these insane, senseless little nighttime raids on a tiny little inconsequential town on the edge of the Rhineland, and we just got the heck shot out of us. And this hand grenade, at least I think it was a hand grenade because I think I saw the spark, went off under my foot. I was running toward the back of a house and a German had thrown the thing. It blew me up, of course, and the fragments of TNT from the grenade, and mud and stuff, got in both my eyes. My eyes were in pretty bad shape, and they became infected. And I'll never forget the day when they took the bandages off and I could see for the first time — light. A joyful moment. And I'll never forget the first time when I was well enough with my good eye to read a newspaper headline, and I thought for a long time that I wouldn't be able to do anything for a long time that required a lot of reading. It was about a year, I guess, before I could read. I was blind for a few weeks. (*Writing the Southwest*)

When Hillerman hit the ground after the explosion, his left foot, ankle, and shinbone were broken, and the sole of his left boot was embedded in his right knee. During a lull in the fighting, a stretcher crew picked him up and began carting his bloodied body away. Suddenly a sniper shot hit one of them, killing the attendant and tossing Hillerman to the ground. Another soldier grabbed hold of his stretcher, and after an accidental dunking in a creek, Hillerman was finally carried to safety.

Tony Hillerman spent the following months in a military hospital in Aix-en-Provence, his body cast the playing surface for what he describes as the world's longest poker game (*Talking Mysteries* 116). Only when the players refused to stop the game for a presidential address did the nurse become so incensed that she temporarily took away their cards. In the end, after a final winning streak which put him ninety dollars "to the good,"

Hillerman shipped out of Marseilles in a hospital convoy and headed back to the United States. When he returned to America Tony found out that his brother Barney had gone AWOL to visit him in the hospital, but arrived just a few hours after his departure.

Hillerman landed in New York in July 1945, and for the first time in his life the farmboy-turned-war-veteran used a telephone. He phoned his mother and sister Margaret, who had taken lodgings in Oklahoma City, to tell them he was on his way home. Despite the instant communication afforded by the telephone, Hillerman's mother was already well aware of her son's movements and activities, for he was a faithful and enthusiastic correspondent during his entire stay abroad. In fact, it was his letters, written with remarkable directness, sincerity, and precision, which were the turning point in Hillerman's eventual emergence as a writer.

Several months before Tony's return from France, in late April, a feature writer for the *Daily Oklahoman* was handed an assignment: Beatrice Stahl was to write an article about a local boy who had received a Silver Star for bravery. There was nothing unusual in this. Like every newspaper, the *Daily Oklahoman* devoted pages every day to recounting both the tragic and heroic fates met by men and women of its community during the war. Beatrice Stahl had done many such articles before, and she launched into this story with gusto and patriotic fervour. However, Stahl discovered that, unlike the other soldiers she had described, the young hero in question, a certain Private First Class Anthony Hillerman, had written reams of heart-wrenching letters to his mother. After reading some of them, Stahl realized that these letters were far more powerful than anything that she might write, and so she wisely chose to quote extensively from them in her article.

On April 24, 1945, a dramatic illustration of a soldier tossing a hand grenade appeared on page 12 of the *Daily Oklahoman*, with the stark headline "He Stood Fearlessly" above, and a picture of Anthony Hillerman below. Here is the article that followed:

One brave man honored another on the day Pfc. Anthony G. Hillerman received his Silver Star. For Hillerman, a fighting man of Oklahoma, was decorated by the hero of Bastogne, who punctuated history with a word.

On the morning of February 12, at an unnamed spot within the Reich, Maj. Gen. Anthony C. McAuliffe, who answered the Nazi demand for surrender with "Nuts!", pinned a Silver Star on the borrowed blouse of Private Hillerman who single-handedly beat off a vicious counterattack on his company's right flank, in another and later engagement.

Tony Hillerman is 19. He was born in Pottawatomie county and has always called Sacred Heart his home. He had finished Konawa high school and entered A&M college when his older brother went into service, and Tony quit school to manage the family's 140 acre farm.

Then came Tony's eighteenth birthday and he decided the army needed him, too. So he landed in France with a glider battalion ground crew on D-Day and later transferred to the infantry. Now both brothers serve in Europe.

It was to his mother, Mrs. Lucy Hillerman and his sister, Margaret Mary, of 709 NW 9, that he wrote on the evening of that big day, Feb. 12.

"This morning I shaved, put on the cleanest clothes I could borrow and they took me back to the rear. There they had a lot of troops in review, a band playing, and a platform with lots of brass on it.

"I went up to the platform and the general, our division commander, (103rd. Inf. Div.) pinned a Silver Star on me, shook my hand, and I went back to the company. . . . It was for something that happened back in January. I'm getting a lot of kidding now, but I'm kinda proud. . . . Don't let the citation worry you. I was just in the right place at the right time."

The order for the Silver Star, read by General McAuliffe that morning, cited this private first class for "magnificent courage" and told a story of daring action during the early hours of 19 January, near an undisclosed town in France.

In the dimness of that dawn, Hillerman, a mortar gunner, was with his company in the midst of battle when a severe enemy counterattack struck on the company's right flank. The concentration of German small arms and mortar fire was so terrific that Hillerman's mortar was knocked out of action at the very beginning of the fight.

His was an important position. Quickly he realized the imminent danger that confronted the whole company, should the enemy break through that spot. So he forgot his own danger, and stayed at his post — armed only with a pistol and hand grenades.

The Nazis came pouring toward him, supported by all that they had. He couldn't tell how many. But it didn't matter now. Somehow he knew they must be stopped. And it was then that Hillerman no longer crouched beside his broken gun. He stood up.

The citation picks up the story: "He stood fearlessly in the face of enemy fire, simultaneously shooting his pistol and throwing hand grenades into the midst of the onrushing foe.

"His utter disregard for his life . . . his gallantry and accuracy of fire, resulted in four enemy dead and the complete disorganization of the hostile attack. Private Hillerman's magnificent courage was in accordance with the highest traditions."

Some of Tony Hillerman's letters give a graphic description of how the boys from home get along over there in what he calls a "strange kind of war." On December 18, he wrote:

"Tonight I'm sitting in an expensive apartment in an overstuffed chair and I've got a deep featherbed waiting in the next room. Of course, I'm plenty dirty. I haven't had my pants or shirt off in over a month. But we're all the same, so it doesn't matter. Tomorrow night I may be sleeping in a foxhole, but tonight I've got a silk bedspread."

December 23: "It looks like we're going to have a white

Christmas after all, and it's a lot like living in a Christmas card. Narrow cobblestone streets, peaked roofs with snow on them. Chimney pots, etc. Everything you could expect to find on a good Hallmark edition.

"We're living in a manger at present. It's not bad, though, stove, plenty of straw. We've been singing a lot of Christmas carols and so forth. It's not like being home for Christmas, but we'll have that next year — all of us.

"In the last town the man of the house came into the kitchen where we were gathered around the stove and sang carols with us. In German, of course. He had a nice looking daughter, too. I liked it there but we had to move on. We always do. So we shook hands with old "pop," kissed Josephine goodbye, put on our packs, and moved on down the road.

"This is a strange life. Today we have a manger, tomorrow perhaps a hotel suite, perhaps a foxhole."

In March, he wrote from a hospital bed in France, where he recovers from shrapnel wounds, sustained in a volunteer patrol.

"I'm plenty proud of my outfit. They're the bravest bunch of men in the world.

"I hope you haven't worried about me. I hope you don't feel sorry for me, either. I don't. I've gotten more out of this war than my scars. I found out just how good a man I am. I learned a lot, and I gained a good deal of self-confidence and self-respect.

"I didn't have to go on that patrol, and I didn't go because I wanted to either. No one does. I can't find words for why we do go on. It's something we learn from watching others we love, do things for us.

"Every time I was in danger, I thought of you praying for me, and you can't realize how much it helped. I wish I could let you know how much I love you all. Tony." (Stahl)

Upon Hillerman's return to Oklahoma, on convalescent furlough, he spent many hours pondering his next move in the world. The war would soon be over, and he had a bum knee, a weak eye, and a handful of medals. He had been enrolled in chemistry before the war, but that no longer seemed suitable. He considered engineering — learning to rebuild the world that had been so terribly shaken. But that wasn't quite right either. He needed a calling, and to his great fortune, he received one. A call. From Beatrice Stahl, who had learned that he was back from Europe and sought him out. It was she who suggested to Tony that he might have a career as a writer, saying that his letters showed a natural flair and grace with language. She was the first writer he had ever met, and this was the first time he had ever considered becoming a writer. But he had always loved reading, and if she, a professional, thought he could do it, then maybe it was worth a try. Imagine, a reporter! In September 1945, using his GI benefits, Tony Hillerman began studying Journalism at the University of Oklahoma. It was the beginning of his first — or is it second? — successful career.

2

In the interim between Hillerman's return from war and his re-enrolment at university, a significant event occurred. Like the publication of his letters, it seemed merely an unusual diversion at the time, but it too was to have a profound impact upon Hillerman's life.

Hillerman spent the summer of 1945 on a sixty-day convalescent furlough back home in Oklahoma. A friend's father supplied oil-drilling equipment to rigs throughout the Southwest, and one day Tony was offered a job driving a truckload of pipe to a distant site. Happy for the adventure, the money, and the moral support, Hillerman gladly accepted. Where was the truck headed? About seven hundred miles due west — near Crownpoint, New Mexico. Navajo country.

Driving through the Navajo Reserve today, a twenty-six-thousand-square-mile territory that overlaps the boundaries of three states, one immediately understands that this is no longer America. In 1945, how much more true this was. Before television. Before the United States was united by an all-consuming mass culture. In 1945, Crownpoint, New Mexico, was, for all intents and purposes, another country — the land of another people, another culture, another history. As Tony Hillerman drove through the reservation, the young world-traveller drank in his new surroundings eagerly. It was his first taste of the air, first sight of the land and smell of the piñons which he would in later years describe so richly for so many readers.

Abruptly, Hillerman slammed on the brakes and brought his wheezing engine to a sudden halt. There, ahead of him on a dusty highway, were the inhabitants of this foreign land. No less than a dozen horses and riders, all dressed in ceremonial attire, were crossing the road, paying him not the slightest attention.

Hillerman watched with fascination as the impressive parade passed him and disappeared behind a boulder. Later, when he stopped to deliver his equipment, he discovered that these Navajos were participating in a ritual curing ceremony, an Enemy Way, being held to cleanse a young soldier back from the war of the taint of his Japanese enemies. The leader of the group had been carrying something aloft, tied to a pole. This was the "stick carrier" delivering the "scalp" to the ceremony.

"Could he attend?" asked Hillerman intrepidly. The driller replied that while strangers did not usually attend such events, if they behaved respectfully they were not unwelcome. So that evening Tony Hillerman wrapped his jacket around him and skirted the nightlong ceremony, watching the comings and goings, noting the seriousness and joyfulness of the event, smelling the burning wood and leaves, examining the stars, the lines of the distant mesas — all sparking a deep sense of admiration and respect, and an urge to learn more about these people, these customs, this land. Though he was only dimly aware of it at the time, Hillerman had fallen deeply in love.

It would be many years before those feelings were expressed. In the meantime Hillerman had a job to do. He had to get his truck back to Oklahoma City. He had to get back to university — he was starting journalism school in just a few weeks. And he had to get back to his family and friends in Oklahoma, to his home.

★   ★   ★   ★

Anthony Grove Hillerman was born on May 27, 1925 (forty years to the day after Dashiell Hammett), in the tiny hamlet of Sacred Heart, located at the extreme eastern edge of Pottawatomie County, Oklahoma. His brother Barney had preceded him by two years, his sister Margaret by four. Along with parents Gus and Lucy, the five Hillermans totalled a little under ten percent of Sacred Heart's population. Gus was coproprietor of the general store, located at the town's only crossroads. The Hillerman family also tilled a small farm of 140 acres.

Dawn at Shiprock, New Mexico.

PHOTO COURTESY TERRENCE MOORE

Pottawatomie, or "Potts" county, was named after the Pottawatomie Indians, who were forcibly resettled there in the mid-nineteenth century. They were among the scores of Indian tribes that had been moved and moved and moved again in the awful years preceding and following the Trail of Tears. Prior to becoming a state, Oklahoma was known as Indian territory and became home to Indians from all across eastern America. Thus, the Pottawatomies were originally from Indiana, and the Seminoles, who were also to be found in Potts county in substantial numbers, had been marched — those who survived — all the way from Florida.

Sacred Heart itself was named after the Benedictine mission established there in 1875 by Father Isidore Robot, who had been sent to these wild lands by his home monastery in the French Pyrenees. Clearing land, living in rude shacks, growing their own food, that first group of five hardy monks was joined in 1885 by an equal number of sisters from the Illinois-based order the Sisters of Mercy. Together these Christian educators ran schools for the local populace, both native and white.

By the time Tony Hillerman was born, the Benedictines had moved north to Shawnee, where they founded a college that still survives today. They left the original site to the Sisters of Mercy in 1909, who continued to run a boarding school and orphanage for Pottawatomie girls. The Benedictine Abbey, which had been modestly rebuilt after a devastating 1901 fire, lay abandoned, quietly creaking and crumbling as the years rolled by.

Tony's mother was Lucy Grove, and his father was Alfred August Hillerman. Though Lucy had spent her earliest years in Iowa, most of her childhood was lived in Norman, Oklahoma, where as a girl her family had homesteaded a claim to 160 acres of prairie. Hillerman recalls her descriptions of that lonely time: "In this woodless landscape, where desiccated cow and buffalo chips were the only source of fuel, she and her brother would sometimes take a wagon ride to a creek where three cottonwoods grew — a nostalgic trip into a childhood enriched by shade trees" (*Hillerman Country* 18).

Sacred Heart, Oklahoma.

PHOTOS COURTESY ANNIE HILLIS

Gus Hillerman had been born in 1875 in Germany and had come to America with his parents as a boy. After spending much of his life in Missouri, he moved to Potts county after the area was opened up to white settlers in 1901. There he met Lucy Grove, and shortly thereafter they were married.

As coproprietor of the community's nucleus — the general store — Gus Hillerman played a major role in the dissemination of news, messages, and goods in and about Sacred Heart. Hillerman's front porch, upon which were placed a couple of wooden benches, was a gathering place for the "good old boys" of the community, who would whittle away both the hours and the benches themselves as they joked, philosophized, and spun yarns. Tony Hillerman recalls that his dad had to replace the benches regularly due to their being whittled away to a toothpick-like fragility during these long sessions. Of these tobacco-chewing farmers, Hillerman recalls, "They were full of B.S., but you couldn't help liking them" (qtd. in Ward 19).

Gus Hillerman had a number of local duties which brought him respect from the community. Quite apart from selling gas, overalls, pig feed, and the thousand other necessities of Oklahoma life, he also served as the town notary public and postmaster. Furthermore, according to Tony, he was among the best bootleg vintners in the state. And finally, like nearly all of his neighbours, he tried valiantly yet with little success to farm.

The soil in Potts county had once been relatively rich, and farming had been a source of food and income for Sacred Heart throughout most of its brief existence. But by the 1930s, the combination of drought, overfarming, and wind had led to a severe erosion of nutrients in the earth. Oklahoma was at the centre of what would become known as the dust bowl. And Potts county, at the centre of Oklahoma, was given the unenviable title of "centre of critical soil erosion in America" (Carr 8).

It was to places like Potts county that Dorothea Lange travelled to take her still haunting photographs for the Resettlement Administration, a national relief agency set up to aid the thousands of rural workers driven from their farmlands. It was to villages like Sacred Heart that James Agee would travel on a similar mission, interviewing locals and documenting their struggles for his extraordinary account of this period, *Let Us Now Praise Famous Men*. And it was Oklahoma that the Joads, John Steinbeck's unforgettable family of destitute and hopeful farmers in *The Grapes of Wrath*, struggled to leave behind as they set out for a new life in California.

And yet at this time Tony was merely a child, and like all children he knew of no other life. There was plenty of hard work to do on the farm, yet while the Hillermans owned no tractor and had very little money, there was apparently always enough to eat. The Hillerman farmhouse was slapped together by Gus from two oil-field shotgun houses. There was an outhouse but no electricity, which was entirely typical, and the children hauled water from the well, although there was never enough for more than a few buckets at a time.

Gus and Lucy were proud Catholics, and they instilled the values of piety, honesty, and responsibility in their children as best they could. Tony Hillerman recalls the atmosphere when he was growing up:

> I can remember being aware of great expectations in our family in terms of standards set. Our name represented people who, when they said they would be somewhere at 8 o'clock, would be there at 8 o'clock. If you made a promise you kept it.
>
> And we were never, hardly ever, punished, except for withdrawal of privileges and an awareness that what we had done did not meet family standards, that it was something that would be tolerated only among white trash. (qtd. in Black 81)

As Adolf Hitler began to receive international attention during his rise to power in the 1930s, Gus Hillerman struggled even more devotedly to teach his children that whatever taunts they might receive, each person was to be judged individually, not as part of a larger stereotyped group.

My dad was German and conscious of being German and very, very ashamed of Hitler. And I think because of that he spent more time than he would have otherwise drumming it into his kids that you don't judge people by anything except how they behave themselves. (qtd. in Carr 9)

When Tony was old enough to be sent to school, his parents decided against the two-room schoolhouse down the road. They considered the teacher there to be "subliterate" (Gorney C2), and instead persuaded the Sisters of Mercy to accept Tony as a day student in their school, St. Mary's Academy. Thus, Tony spent his first eight grades in school as one of a very few local boys in a Catholic school for Pottawatomie Indian girls.

Although a place was made for the boys in the classrooms, they were strictly separated from the girls at other times. The local boys were never allowed to play with the girls, or otherwise socialize with them. "The nuns forgave us for not being [Indians]," Tony remembers, "but they never forgave us for not being girls" (qtd. in Ward 19). Although he jokes about it now, it was not always easy to be so singled out. Long before the term "reverse discrimination" gained currency, Tony Hillerman learned what it felt like to be discriminated against for being white and male. It was a lesson in prejudice he would never forget.

As a boy, Hillerman was naturally attracted to the one historically interesting local site — the ruins of the Benedictine Abbey, which offered innumerable niches and vistas for the young imagination to work upon. In an article for *Oklahoma Today*, written more than fifty years after he had left Sacred Heart, Hillerman recalled his childhood there.

It's ironic that the same place from which you longed to escape as a teen-ager should call to you a half-century later. For me, that place is Sacred Heart, then a dying cotton gin and farm community in the poor end of Pottawatomie County and now a ghost town. I was born there in 1925, played in the gin pond and in the Mountains of rotting cotton hulls and grew up a country boy — identifying then and always with hard-working red-neck folks.

There's not much there now[,] there wasn't much even when I was a boy. The big old abbey the Benedictine monks had built in the 1870s had been erased by fire in 1901, along with the school they and the Sisters of Mercy had established to educate Pottawatomie Indians boys and girls. The abbey had been rebuilt, a three-story brick "U" which would have looked at home in northern France, and the Sisters had replaced their school with a rambling two-storey frame building with porches everywhere. But when I was a child the abbey was virtually deserted — the boys school moved to Shawnee to become St. Gregory's College — and no one lived there but our parish priest.

The church we attended is still there, still a landmark crowning Bald Hill. It is much smaller now than I remembered it from my days as an altar boy. And the view has changed, too. The new abbey under the hill is gone, demolished after an earthquake cracked its walls. So is St. Mary's Academy, where I went as one of a tiny minority of farm boys in a boarding school for Pottawatomie girls. But the cemetery is there, with my mother and father, and uncles, aunts and cousins, and what's left of Zeller's pear orchard, and the stone buildings which once housed a general store and a service station, and a few modest houses. And from Sacred Heart Church atop Bald Hill, the prairie hills and the wooded creeks roll away to the horizon — the same beauty I remember from boyhood. ("Tony Hillerman Remembers Sacred Heart")

From an early age, Tony had enjoyed hearing his mother tell him stories and read to him from books. But books were hard to come by and there was no library within miles. So Tony often sent away to the state library for books. The process was both slow and imprecise, as the list of books he requested — *Captain*

Blood, Death on Horseback, and other similar novels — was not always looked upon favourably by the distant librarians.

About three weeks later the books would arrive, and there'd be a form letter on top which would say: "Dear library patron, we are sorry to inform you that the books you have ordered are not on our shelves at this time. We have taken the liberty of substituting others which we feel will satisfy your interests." And then of course in the package would be the history of the Masonic order in Oklahoma, and *Conquests of Peru*, and so forth. And as a result you got sort of a broad education. (*Writing the Southwest*)

Yet occasionally, an inattentive clerk might let one of those tantalizingly immoral yet heroic tales get through. And there were other means of getting hold of juicy stories — in the *Saturday Evening Post*, for example, which Tony delivered for a period. It was there that he first encountered the stories of Arthur Upfield, the author whose now-forgotten work was to have the greatest literary influence upon Tony Hillerman the novelist.

Surprisingly, it was only when a reviewer of one of Hillerman's early Leaphorn novels suggested the link to Upfield in print that Hillerman recalled his youthful passion for the Australian detective novelist. In fact, Upfield's protagonist was a half-breed policeman who used his knowledge of aboriginal culture and territory to solve crimes in the outback. Upfield also wrote passionate descriptive passages in which he brought to life that dry, forbidding landscape for readers in distant, more temperate climes. Thus, as a boy, Tony Hillerman encountered and absorbed the work of a writer whose aims and passions would prove similar to his own.

Another early source of reading material, and an introduction to a legion of fascinating faraway worlds, was the cache of books the Hillerman brothers discovered in the ruins of the abbey. When Tony was twelve, and Barney fourteen, they asked for and received permission from the parish priest to catalogue the entire collection of books, long since abandoned by the Benedictine Brothers. The Hillerman brothers spent countless hours lounging, reading, organizing, and trying to decipher the dusty library, which included books in German, French, and Latin, works by Plutarch and Washington Irving, and *Lives of the Saints*. Between the erratic mailings from the state library and the haphazard and multilingual collection in the old abbey, Tony Hillerman acquired a genuinely catholic knowledge of history and literature. But perhaps his most important acquisition was a deeply rooted love of reading, a love which would shape his entire life.

Of course, the life of a farmboy, no matter how literate and precocious he may be, is nonetheless filled with a wide assortment of other activities, including a perennial favourite: the casual mocking of the town boys. Tony Hillerman recalls his participation in this pastime:

The town boys got their hair cut in barber shops, knew how to shoot pool, didn't carry their lunch in sacks, wore belt pants and low-cuts instead of overalls and work shoes, had spending money, knew about calling people on telephones, and were otherwise urbane and sophisticated. We were better rifle shots, better at riding horses, could endure hot hours feeding the hay baler, and, until we tried it, were better at fistfighting. Thus the them-and-us division of my childhood was totally without racial-ethnic lines. Our Seminole and Pottawatomie Indian neighbors were part of Us, fellow barbarians teamed against Them, the town-boy Greeks. . . .

I have since become old enough to know the above is mostly nonsense. Konawa, Oklahoma (home of the town boys), with its main street, two banks, drugstore, ice house, theater where a movie was shown every Saturday, and competitive pool halls, wasn't much more urbane than Sacred Heart, Oklahoma, the crossroads with a filling station and cotton gin, which was the center of our country-boy universe. (*Talking Mysteries* 24)

And yet, when Tony left St. Mary's Academy to take the rickety school bus into town to attend Konawa High School in grade nine, he was unable to completely shake his disdain and antagonisms. When one of the stars of the high school football team, an Indian with a Seminole name, was unceremoniously dumped from the squad and expelled from school because a teammate swore that the Indian's one Negro great-grandparent made him unfit company, Hillerman was disgusted and hurt. There was no Negro high school in the region, and the boy was forced to abandon his education there and then. Jim Thorpe, the legendary Indian athlete and football player, had been educated at Sacred Heart a generation earlier, giving native athletes a certain status, but it would be a long time before Jackie Robinson would break the colour barrier in professional sports. Hillerman was fast reaching the age when a boy wants to rebel, to leave home and discover the world on his own, to have adventures beyond the scope of his childhood home. Incidents like these confirmed to Hillerman that he wanted to explore the world. Maybe there were other, better, places?

3

At the age of sixteen Tony Hillerman graduated from Konawa High School. He had been Class Historian during his final year, but neither this honour nor the adolescent social life truly satisfied his yearnings. He wanted more out of life than Sacred Heart, or even Konawa, could offer. And, for the worst of all possible reasons, it appeared that significant changes were imminent. For in 1941, the year before Tony graduated, Gus Hillerman died of a heart condition on Christmas Day. "He literally worked himself to death between the store and the farm," Tony recalls (*Talking Mysteries* 115). Despite his ailments, Gus Hillerman had remained highly respected in the local community. He wrote letters for illiterate neighbours, offered credit at his store, and represented disenfranchised sharecroppers in negotiations with the county commissioners. His death was a major blow to the family's spirits and fortunes.

After his father's death, Tony finished high school, but it was clear the family would soon be undergoing dramatic changes. The war was in full swing in Europe and Barney was keen to enlist. Lucy and Margaret decided to try to keep the farm alive, while the youngest and most bookish of the three children, Tony, went to college. "My goal was to get off the farm. Anything that got you off the farm was a success," Tony later recalled about those teenage years (qtd. in Smith 23).

According to Tony's reminiscences, he was practically the first Konawa High graduate to ever attend college. Yet this anecdote, like many others the inveterate storyteller has related over the years, is somewhat fanciful. In fact, despite its remote location and relative poverty, Konawa High had a remarkably consistent record of sending well over fifty percent of its students to college every year. It also featured a school band ranked among the top in the nation. Hillerman's schooling in Konawa certainly helped to prepare him for Oklahoma State, where he ended up in the fall of 1942.

Nobody in Hillerman's family had ever been to university, and neither Lucy nor Tony's siblings were very sure of when the semester even started. By the time Tony arrived at the school's administrative building requesting admittance, classes had already been in session for ten days. Oklahoma State was more or less familiar with such situations, however, and the seventeen-year-old student was quickly enrolled in chemistry, provided with a class schedule, and given a list of books to buy. After paying for his semester's tuition and buying his books, Tony, who had been given the family savings to get started, had only enough money left for his first month's rent.

Life at university was strange and exciting for the keen-eyed young bumpkin. He met students from across the state, and the country. When, in the years that followed, he was to become a successful author, Hillerman's thoughts would often turn back to this era, to the characters he befriended, to the coming of age of a young farmboy. He has said many times that he hopes to write a sort of redneck *Catcher in the Rye* set in Oklahoma, using his friends as models. Once he even described what those characters would be like:

There's one who traps squirrels in the city park to get a little protein in his diet. I know hard times have not really reached America when I see the ducks and geese on the (University of New Mexico) pond.

One of the young men would be relatively sophisticated, kicked out of Georgia Tech, disowned by an affluent Southern family.

He survived by selling his wardrobe. For years I had one of his sport coats. And he had 12 shirts. I'd never known anyone who had 12 shirts.

Another was a devout Baptist. The only thing we boys had

in common was abject poverty and ambition. (qtd. in Black
B1)

Hillerman soon found a room for rent, or rather a half a room.
He shared the room, and out of necessity, the room's one bed,
with another equally impecunious student from Oklahoma City.
They paid fifteen dollars a month for the room, located in a
ramshackle rooming house. The teenagers were, however, per-
mitted a certain leeway in meeting their payment schedule, so
long as they would regularly play bridge with the elderly female
proprietor.

Before long Tony had assumed four part-time jobs in order to
ensure a roof over his head and food in his belly. Not surprisingly,
his schoolwork suffered as a result. By the time his second
semester began, his marks were dropping and even his handful
of part-time jobs was inadequate to cover both tuition costs and
living expenses. Barney had enlisted and gone off to Europe to
serve as a glider mechanic. His mother and sister were having
difficulty maintaining the farm. The answer seemed clear —
Tony abandoned his studies and went back to Sacred Heart.
Although he could not know that within three years he would
be returning to a different university as an altogether different
man, he did know that Sacred Heart was no longer big enough
for his ambitions. The writing was on the wall — as soon as it
could be arranged, the family sold off all but a small parcel of
the farm, along with the farm equipment and livestock. Lucy
Hillerman found a job in Oklahoma City in the laundry room
of a hospital, and she and Margaret took an apartment in the city.
Tony, his feet carrying him as fast as he could make them, hurried
down to the recruiting office and signed up for the war.

★   ★   ★   ★

The second time Tony Hillerman enrolled in university, in 1945,
everything had changed. He was no longer enrolled in Chemistry but in Journalism. He was no longer at Oklahoma State but

at the more prestigious University of Oklahoma in Norman, his mother's childhood home. He was no longer a teenage boy longing for adventure but a veteran soldier with a Bronze Star, a Silver Star, and a Purple Heart. He was no longer a fresh-faced country bumpkin, but a worldly young man with a bum knee, a patch over his eye, and memories of suffering, tragedy, and death lying just below the surface of his restrained smile. He was no longer in need of four part-time jobs to pay for half a flea-ridden bed; he was a veteran, and his GI benefits covered the costs of his schooling.

And the world had changed too, all around him. Suddenly, in the shifting framework of the postwar world, anything seemed possible. A writer? Why not? Could it be harder than being a soldier? Unlikely. And there was a whole world to write about. So much to see, so much to say. So many things that needed investigation and explanation, that needed the sharp eye of an observer and the sharp pen of a skilled writer to translate into language, to publish in books, in magazines, in newspapers, so that others could read and discover and feel them. All across America there was a vital energy coursing through the nation, through the hearts of its citizens. Some resisted it. Some were afraid of it. Some condemned it. But Tony Hillerman embraced it, finding in his new vocation the potential to unlock its secrets, and his own.

At the end of war, American colleges were flooded with GIs seeking to take advantage of their generous veterans benefits. Hillerman was one of uncounted veterans who were able to obtain a university degree that would most certainly have been economically unattainable before the war. "Guys like me couldn't go to school," observed Hillerman. "College was for the privileged class" (qtd. in Smith 23). After the war, many of them were in school only because they didn't know where else to go, or because it was a good place to meet girls, or both. Yet even among this crowd of bustling young men, Tony Hillerman soon distinguished himself as an unusual character. In the spring of 1947 he began writing articles for the university's humour magazine, *The Covered Wagon*. A few months later, at the outset of the winter semester of 1947–48, Hillerman took the helm of the magazine and instantly created a controversy with an outspoken piece attacking student drunkenness. The article, which made little pretense at humour, stressed that while social drinking might be acceptable, the loutish obscenities which accompanied pie-eyed alcoholic oblivion were disgusting and immoral. This condemnation of the most popular university pastime was received with much indignation and outrage by the student populace. Although the fuss soon blew over, Hillerman was reminded of it in the student yearbook when his arrival at *The Covered Wagon* was thus described:

> Intent on making a success of the *Wagon* and saving souls at the same time, Hillerman recognized early the folly of doing two jobs at once. He agreed with the WCTU [Women's Christian Temperance Union] that he would leave the souls to them and he, in turn, would take complete charge of the magazine. That arrangement continued in effect until Hillerman crossed the plank with the senior class in June. (*Sooner Yearbook* 305)

Hillerman's tirade, though unprovoked, was not out of character for the lifelong teetotaler. Hillermans had, in fact, been prominent in the fight for prohibition in Oklahoma, and despite his father's winemaking, the family abhorrence of drunkenness was impressed upon Tony throughout his childhood. This theme would reappear in his later fiction, notably in *Coyote Waits*, in which the crime is precipitated by whiskey, and the old Navajo storyteller who commits the murder delivers an anti-drinking speech from the witness stand. Although Hillerman had incurred the wrath of a thirsty student population, the yearbook went on to praise Hillerman's professional handling of the magazine: "He sought and obtained the best writing talent on the campus, stealing from the *Daily* such esteemed penmen as Larry Grove . . ." (305). But Tony was not the only Hillerman toiling for the *Wagon*. His brother Barney, who was also enrolled at

*Photographs from the
University of Oklahoma
yearbook for 1947–48, including
Hillerman as editor of the
college humour magazine,
"The Covered Wagon."*

U of O in Geology, had recently discovered photography, and contributed his own work to the magazine regularly. Remarkably, within months of returning from the war, each of these two brothers had found his vocation. Tony would become a journalist, editor, and author, while Barney would spend his entire professional life as a freelance photographer. The two brothers would not work together again for almost fifty years, when they were contracted to write and photograph the Four Corners region — an area overlapping parts of New Mexico, Arizona, Colorado and Utah — in a lovely book called *Hillerman Country*, published in 1991.

The yearbook concluded its tribute to *The Covered Wagon* with another jab at its editor: " 'You just don't realize what a job it is,' Hillerman said, 'to separate the grain from the chaff,' but he always seemed to get the chaff to the printers in time for the deadline" (305).

Quite apart from the antics at the magazine, Hillerman was busy working at his journalism degree. Among his most important mentors was Grace Ray, who taught Hillerman "to say precisely and exactly what one intended to say with no wasted words" (Sandstrom 4). By 1948 he had completed all of the necessary prerequisites for graduation. Yet his ambitions were no longer focused exclusively on working as a writer. He had another ambition entirely, which was filled shortly after his graduation when he and Marie Unzner were married.

Marie Elizabeth Unzner was a Phi Beta Kappa Bacteriology major when she met Tony Hillerman at a university sock-hop. Like him she was friendly and generous, yet somewhat shy. Like Hillerman, too, she was from a devout Oklahoman family of German descent. Hailing from Shawnee, some thirty-five miles to the east, Marie had entered the University of Oklahoma in 1945 and served in the spring of 1947 as president of Newman Hall, a dormitory run by the Sisters of Divine Providence for Catholic girls with excellent academic records. She and Tony were engaged soon after they met, and were married on August 16, 1948.

4

In 1948 Tony Hillerman was still only twenty-three years old. Yet he was now married, a university graduate, and a budding freelance journalist. Just out of school, Hillerman began searching for work. Within weeks, his big break arrived. He obtained a job writing! True, he was only writing radio ad copy for Cain's Better Coffee and Purina Pig Chow, but it was a job nonetheless. And it would be a snap. Or so he thought at first. But, as he is fond of recalling when speaking of his inauspicious debut, "It was the most taxing writing assignment I have ever had" (qtd. in Holt 6–7). The young scribe was expected to create three different commercials each and every day for a broadcast that began at 6 a.m. Not quite what a romantic young author dreams of. In fact, Hillerman lasted all of a week in this position, but before long he had managed to find a real job, as a real reporter, on a small-town weekly. So in June, he and Marie packed their bags and headed west, towards Borger, Texas, the "carbon black capital of the world" (qtd. in Holt 7).

Borger is a small industrial community in the Texas panhandle, northeast of Amarillo and less than a hundred miles from the Oklahoma border. Oil was flowing from wells being sunk throughout the area, and Borger's population had mushroomed after the war, as young men poured into town to work on the rigs. The result was an atmosphere not unlike the imaginary Wild West, as the plentiful supply of money, alcohol, and testosterone combined to keep the local sheriff's brigade on their toes. This was not the place for a nervous, school-trained reporter, but for Tony Hillerman, who learned how to write at school but had learned about people and violence elsewhere in his young life, Borger held nothing but fascination. "I loved it," Hillerman exclaims:

It was boomtown in the middle of oil country, carbon-black from oil and gas wells, overcrowded with drillers, plenty of fights, and no decent housing. Marie and I were newlyweds. We lived in a kind of a box on an alley, behind a frame bungalow. (Bernell and Karni 3)

Hillerman was assigned the police beat, which he took to with relish.

The only civic monument was a bullet hole in the post office wall where Ace Borger, the first mayor and founder of the town, had been shot to death by a dissident policeman. The town, new as it was, had already had martial law. Texas Rangers had come in and taken over to try and bring some order to the place. It was a great place to break in as a police reporter. It had every crime in the books. (*Writing the Southwest*)

The Borger *News Herald* was published by J.C. Phillips, who was equally proud to have founded the first Anti-Communist League. The paper itself was, in Hillerman's words, "one of the worst in Christendom" (qtd. in Ward 19), yet it printed up Hillerman's stories and assigned him new ones each day. He learned how to write, but he also learned about the struggles and tragedies that led to his assignments. Very little escaped his attention. "[W]ithin six months I covered every offense listed in the Old Testament and several mentioned only in Krafft-Ebing" (qtd. in Holt 7).

By the end of the year, Hillerman had been promoted to city editor, but Borger's romance was beginning to fade for both him and Marie. They missed their friends and family, and when Hillerman was offered a job as news editor at the Lawton *Morning Press*, working with friends back in Oklahoma, he and Marie jumped at it.

*   *   *   *

During the next four years, Tony Hillerman honed his skills as one of the most intrepid and insightful young reporters in the state. During his year and a half in Lawton, he rose from news editor to city editor, learning the many ins and outs of the news business en route. As his abilities grew, so did his still modest reputation, though he had gained enough credibility by June 1950 to garner a position with United Press International, one of the major news bureaus in America. Perhaps the most significant aspect of this new job was that it meant living and working in the capital, Oklahoma City. For a reporter, this was the real thing. His first job was as a simple reporter, assigned to covering the minor, rural events in Oklahoma, but he soon moved up to become editor of upi radio news reports. From there, Hillerman was finally named state capitol reporter for upi, responsible for covering state politics. Hillerman was comparatively young for this assignment, particularly as he found himself working side by side with grizzled veterans of countless election campaigns and political scandals. Yet he was both a keen observer and a skilled journalist, and with youthful enthusiasm he was able to make up for what he may have lacked in experience.

During this time, Hillerman was cited with a special newspaperman's award for a series of articles reporting on corruption in the Oklahoma Emergency Relief Agency. This series led to the removal of the agency's director and major reforms in the handling and distribution of funds. But while there were occasional highlights such as this, for the most part, the political reporter's role was simply to report and report, day in and day out, on the activities of the legislature. He later recalled to one interviewer that he and his partner at upi had each churned out six thousand words on an average day, and as many as ten thousand when there was a major crisis. The stories were endless, the deadlines relentless, and over time this rigorousness turned Tony Hillerman into an extremely capable journalist.

Despite his success in his home state, Tony Hillerman continued to yearn for wider pastures. He had never forgotten that trip, years earlier, when he had hauled a truckload of pipe out to New

Mexico, to the Navajo Reservation. So in October 1952, Hillerman transferred to Santa Fe, the capital city of New Mexico, where he was appointed UPI bureau chief. He was the youngest bureau chief in the United States.

Despite his exclusively journalistic writing activities, Hillerman had begun dreaming of writing fiction, of writing, in fact, the Great American Novel. And Santa Fe, one of the most beautiful cities in America, with its magnificent adobe buildings and widespread Mexican, Hopi, Navajo, Pueblo, and Spanish influences, turned out to have been a very good choice for a writer with such lofty ambitions.

The old Santa Fe art colony, and writer's colony, was on its last legs; the people who made the city famous were past their prime when I got there. But Witter Bynner was still there, and a good many other famous folks were still writing or painting or whatever they did. It was an interesting place for a young guy to be who wanted to be a writer. (*Writing the Southwest*)

At this time, though, Hillerman was still many years away from attempting that long-dreamt-of novel. In the meantime, he was a journalist, and an extremely good one at that. His rise through the ranks was as inexorable, in retrospect, as that of a general or president. And it was due, most certainly, to Hillerman's moral integrity, his fairness, and his understanding of human psychology, at least as much as it was to his unquestionable skills as a writer.

In April 1954 Hillerman was promoted from Santa Fe bureau chief to New Mexico editor for UPI. But he had been four years with UPI, and while the bureau offered certain opportunities, it also guaranteed certain limitations on the kinds of articles that could be written, and their length. Only two months later, in June, Hillerman left UPI and moved to the most important daily paper in the state, the Santa Fe *New Mexican*, where he hoped he could further develop his political writing. The *New Mexican* was

PHOTO COURTESY CENTER FOR SOUTHWEST RESEARCH

NO. 000-505-0001

44

to become Hillerman's true journalistic home. It was there that he would become a mature journalist with a major platform from which to work. The Santa Fe *New Mexican* already had progressive political leanings when Hillerman arrived, and during his extended stay at the newspaper those tendencies increased. For Hillerman never believed, as is so common among American journalists, that a reporter could be an impartial observer, a simple cipher who informs the public of a situation but plays no role in it himself. This notion is a convenient rationalization which allows reporters to avoid making difficult choices and responding to the considerable demands of their own consciences when reporting. Hillerman knew from the outset that because a reporter is engaged with his subject by the very act of reporting on it, a moral position is essential to guide him in his telling of the story. Not surprisingly, then, Tony Hillerman was eventually assigned the task of writing editorials for the *New Mexican*, which suited his disposition admirably. Over the eight years following his hiring in 1954, Hillerman rose from political reporter to city editor, to managing editor, and finally to executive editor.

As he had done in Oklahoma, Hillerman sought, like any good investigative reporter and engaged citizen, to publicize corruption and mismanagement in government. In his early days at the *New Mexican* he helped expose massive systematized fraud in the New Mexico National Guard, for which he continued to receive condemnation from certain quarters for years afterward. Later he would win a host of awards from the New Mexico Press Association, among them Best News Story in both 1961 and 1962, and Best Editorial in 1962. Yet Hillerman also worked with a highly skilled staff at the *New Mexican*. Among his writers were Oliver La Farge, whose novel *Laughing Boy* (1930), about a young Navajo, had been awarded a Pulitzer Prize, and Winfield Townley Scott, who had won the National Book Award for poetry.

Yet even this remarkable success began to turn sour for Hillerman. He was in his late thirties and had already achieved everything that a journalist could hope to achieve. He had financial stability, respect from his peers, a powerful position from which to effect change — and yet he was growing restless. Was this everything?

As editor of the Santa Fe *New Mexican*, Hillerman was regularly clocking six-and-a-half-day, tension-filled work weeks. Even the most dedicated journalists eventually burn out, however, and Hillerman was no exception. Indeed, by 1962, Hillerman had been a journalist for nearly fifteen years, during which time he had learned how to relate "just the facts." He had related the facts of murders, robberies, and crimes of all kinds; the facts of trials and elections and legislative battles and community heroes; the facts of rises to power and falls from grace; the facts of every trial, tribulation, terror, and truancy known to New Mexicans and Oklahomans, and he was coming to the end of his capacity for fact-telling. Yet, as Hillerman explains, "at the same time the yen builds to work in something more malleable than hard fact, an urge grows to try to deal with the meaning of all this" (*Talking Mysteries* 29). For Tony Hillerman, that urge would eventually lead him to telling a story without facts, an imaginary yet meaningful story, and he would prove to be even better at this kind of storytelling than he was at reporting.

5

Though the time had arrived for Tony Hillerman to "try to make sense" of his lifetime of observations and actions, he did not yet feel ready to attempt the grandiose American novel he was dreaming of. A transitional period was needed. So, in 1962, to the surprise of many of his admirers and peers in the world of journalism, the executive editor of the Santa Fe *New Mexican* quit and went back to school to study English literature.

Of all the career moves from one paper to another, from one position to another, from one beat to another, nothing in Hillerman's professional life can be compared to the raw courage required of him to choose, at the age of thirty-seven, to give up a successful career and, with a large family to support, embark on the perilous and possibly impecunious pursuit of learning to write fiction. Hillerman ascribes most of the strength necessary to carry through with this resolve to his wife, whose encouragement was unflagging, though he himself doubted the wisdom of this course of action. "[I]f it hadn't been for the encouragement of my wife, Marie," he admits, ". . . I never would have risked it" (qtd. in Holt 7). Yet there were stories Hillerman wanted to tell which could be expressed in no other way — he had to give it a try.

> When all this was happening to me, I was thirty-eight. Marie and I had five children and had been living in Santa Fe, where I was editor of *The New Mexican*. . . . We decided it was time for a change. I resigned. We moved to Albuquerque. I enrolled as a graduate student in English. . . .
>
> The terrible moment had arrived. Naked and exposed. Nothing left to hide behind. No more excuses (or grocery

money). Either you can write fiction or you can't. (*Talking Mysteries* 29)

The speed with which Tony Hillerman's career had evolved was matched by the constant growth of his family. By 1962 Tony and Marie had three daughters and two sons. Anne was the eldest and the only one of the couple's children who was not adopted. Her siblings were Janet, Anthony (Tony Jr.), Monica, and Stephen. In 1963 the family would reach its full size with the adoption of their third son, Daniel.

In January 1963, Hillerman began classes at the University of New Mexico, enrolled as a master's candidate in English. The campus was then, much as it is today, a large block of beautifully designed land in eastern Albuquerque, off the city's main traffic artery, Central Avenue. Albuquerque itself, located approximately sixty miles southwest of Santa Fe, is far less picturesque and self-consciously beautiful than that romantic town. Yet Santa Fe had become somewhat tired for Hillerman.

It was a great place to live, but by the '60s Santa Fe was beginning to attract the self-anointed artists and poets and the dilettantes and the people that I don't particularly like. I was ready to move on. I wanted to start writing a novel but I thought I needed to improve my education. (qtd. in Reid F1)

Albuquerque has always been something of a dark sister to the fairer Santa Fe. Today there are factories and poor neighbourhoods in Albuquerque, and run-down shops and theatres, just as there were in 1963. So the move from Santa Fe involved even more than Tony Hillerman's career shift — it meant a change for the entire family, away from the scenic, artist-filled capital city to a worker's city, a student's city, to a place where Tony Hillerman, still the good old boy at heart, felt much more at home.

Hillerman could not, of course, have given up working entirely. As always, there were bills to pay, and in this case a new house to buy as well, which he and Marie purchased in February. The house was a modest detached brick home located in a quiet residential area at the edge of town, to the east, a couple of miles from the university. So to make ends meet, Hillerman landed what was probably the most unusual part-time job for a grad student in UNM's history: he was hired as a special assistant to Tom Popejoy, the president of the university. Hillerman was, in reality, a high-level troubleshooter who ran from taking notes in classes on Milton and Kafka to sorting out tangles between the university and any number of important individuals and institutions with whom it came into conflict. Hillerman describes himself as having been a "handyman, writer, caddy, [and] doer of undignified political deeds" (*Talking Mysteries* 29).

Popejoy hired Hillerman largely because of Hillerman's distinguished record as editor of the *New Mexican* in supporting liberal causes, including outspoken support for state funding of the University of New Mexico. Tom Popejoy recognized that Hillerman's diplomatic skills, his knowledge of and experience dealing with VIPs, and his plain common sense would make him a valuable asset to the university.

> My job was to do whatever needed to be done, and there were times when [Popejoy] needed some pretty unusual things done. As an example, one day he said to me, "Tony, you're going to get a call from a county sheriff. He's got to have twenty-four mattresses in a hurry without any publicity." Well, I'd been around New Mexico politics for quite a while. I knew this particular sheriff was also the brother of a county chairman who had considerable influence with a couple of state senators. When he called, I told him we had what he wanted, just send a truck over. Later we cashed in those mattresses on two crucial legislative votes for establishing a medical school at UNM.

. . . .

> They'd had a little jail riot and burned up all of his [mattresses]. He didn't want it known, and he didn't have

49

Tony Hillerman, 1977.

the money to buy any more because his budget was overspent. So we gave him twenty-four old Peace Corps mattresses that had been stored in the basement of Hokona Hall. (Bernell and Karni 5–6)

On another occasion, Hillerman had to go to Ecuador in order to bail out of trouble a UNM student who had been detained by the local constabulary.

Although Hillerman knew pretty much all there was to know about news reporting, he had not had the opportunity to educate himself to his satisfaction with respect to the history of English literature. Thus one of his primary purposes in returning to school was to lay the foundation he felt he was lacking, in preparation for attempting his novel.

I'd never studied Shakespeare or Milton, and I'd heard great things about the staff [at UNM] . . . Edith Buchanan, Katherine Simons, and the young woman who taught Chaucer (Ellen Spolsky). Before writing, I wanted to study literature at its roots. (Bernell and Karni 5)

Hillerman's M.A. thesis was written under the direction of Morris Friedman, a UNM professor whom Hillerman credits as having been responsible for much of his development as a writer.

He was an excellent teacher, a fine writer. I learned a tremendous amount from him, the skills I needed. Technique. His encouragement meant a great deal to me in terms of confidence. When Friedman accepted me as an equal and said I was talented, I knew I was talented. . . . I'd been doing a certain kind of writing. I knew I was a competent journalist, but for someone of his caliber to say I was good in another way was very reassuring. (Bernell and Karni 6)

The methodology chosen for Hillerman's thesis was unusual, but highly fruitful. Friedman and Hillerman decided that instead

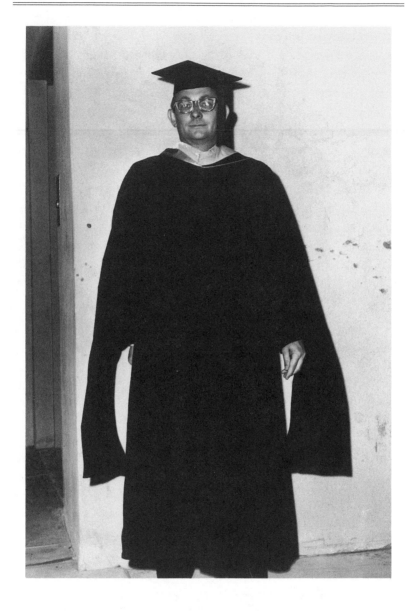

Graduation, 1966, University of New Mexico.

PHOTO COURTESY UNIVERSITY OF NEW MEXICO ARCHIVES

of researching and writing on one particular subject, Hillerman ought to write several longer essays on popular topics which might then be sold to magazines. And so Hillerman wrote a handful of articles on a wide range of subjects. Over the course of the next five years, all of the essays were published in various magazines, and eventually, in 1973, they were collected in a book titled *The Great Taos Bank Robbery, and Other Indian Country Affairs*.

One of these stories deserves particular attention. It was published in the January 1966 issue of *True: The Man's Magazine*, under the title "The Black Death." *True* was a sort of *Playboy* without the naked women, and so, not surprisingly, it has long since disappeared. But in the early sixties, *True* was a reasonably good magazine, and it published several of Hillerman's articles. "The Black Death," which had originally been called "We All Fall Down," was a fascinating and extensively researched investigation of the continued presence of the bubonic plague in the Southwest, and of occasional epidemics which still hit rural desert communities. The story focused upon the work of a doctor who was attempting to document and eradicate the disease. When Hillerman submitted the story to *True*, the editors found the subject very appealing, but felt that Hillerman's treatment was too tame. He was asked to spice it up a bit, by casting the entire piece in the form of a detective novel. Hillerman balked at first, but eventually agreed and rewrote the story as a tale of medical sleuthing. For all this effort, he received $1,000 when the piece was finally published. But he had also acquired something else: a taste — bitter at first, but a taste nonetheless — of the possibilities inherent in the mystery genre.

By December of 1963, Hillerman had completed his academic requirements and would shortly be awarded a Master of Arts degree in English. As was his custom, he wasted no time in finding new opportunities for himself. In fact, just days into 1964 Hillerman was hired by the Department of Journalism at UNM as an associate professor. Although he had never taught a class in his life, Hillerman's wit, experience, and compassion immediately made him a highly regarded teacher. Just two and a half years later, in June of 1966, he was elected chair of the department. His rise from grad student in 1963 to department chair in 1966 must certainly rate as one of the most rapid ascents through the ranks of academia in history.

Hillerman enjoyed teaching. He enjoyed the opportunity to explain to enthusiastic youngsters what he felt was important in journalism — the commitment to fairness, justice, clarity. During his stay at UNM, which would last for more than twenty years, Hillerman taught, among other courses, News Writing and Reporting, Editorial Writing, Mass Media as a Social Force, Magazine Writing, Intermediate Reporting, Advanced Reporting, and Creative Writing.

Tony Hillerman remained chair of the Journalism Department until 1974, a total of eight years. Just as at the *New Mexican*, he had risen swiftly to the top of his field, and stayed there. No doubt Hillerman used his political acuity to retain his position, yet he exercised that acuity for the benefit of all, which is why he remained at the top as long as he felt comfortable there. As at the *New Mexican*, it was Tony Hillerman's own temperament, rather than external pressures, which led him to resign his post. Yet unlike the occasion when he had resigned from the editorship of the *New Mexican* to pursue a dream, by the time Hillerman stepped down from his academic chairmanship, he had already realized a large part of that dream. It was now his intention to pursue it as far as it could lead him. Though he had already experienced modest success as a novelist, it was here that Tony Hillerman truly committed himself to his third career.

6

For years Tony Hillerman had been dreaming — one of those half-hearted dreams which may or may not be realized eventually, but which never go away either — of writing a novel. Despite having been elected chair of his department in 1966, he was determined to try his hand at realizing that dream. After all, that was why he had left journalism in the first place, wasn't it? So, gradually, he began to look for a story to tell. He already knew what his *big* story would be, his Great American Novel: that would be a sort of *War and Peace* in the Southwest, a grandiose tale of political intrigue and psychological drama, set in a state capital and centred on the investigations of a young political reporter. That story had existed in Hillerman's head nearly as long as the idea of writing itself. But perhaps for that reason, when it came time to write it, to tackle this enormous, all-encompassing American morality tale, Hillerman hesitated. Perhaps he wasn't ready for the Big Book. Perhaps he needed to practise on something easier, something less grandiose, less close to his dreams. He would write another novel first. An easier novel. Something to cut his teeth on. But what?

Certain aspects of the book were givens. Hillerman knew that he wanted to write a detective story. He had been reading Ross Macdonald, Graham Greene, Eric Ambler, and Raymond Chandler, and these writers had taught him just how flexible, accommodating, and effective the form could be. Macdonald, Hillerman later said, "taught every one of us that, given enough skill with metaphorical language, one plot is all you ever need for as many books as you want to write" (*Talking Mysteries* 27). And of these great writers in general, he had learned that "[t]hey took the mystery form and made a novel out of it and ground whatever axe they wanted to grind" (*Talking Mysteries* 47). To Hillerman, mystery novels, crime novels, detective novels, these lurid tales of murder and intrigue which were often dismissed by serious literary critics as pulp fiction, were filled with skilled writing. It was natural that Hillerman, a country boy by birth, hard-nosed journalist by training, and idealist by inclination, should be attracted to detective fiction, because it is precisely in the work of hard-boiled authors like Raymond Chandler and Ross Macdonald that one finds the fictive correlative to journalism; they share the same earthiness, the same determination to get to the heart of any issue with concise language. Detective fiction simply allows the imagination to play a little further afield, to employ metaphors, to embrace the poetic. But many of the goals are the same. And the subject matter — the psychology of people affected by (or in love with) violence and dishonesty, and finally the futility of their contortions in the hands of fate — belongs equally to the crime reporter and the crime novelist. Just as Weegee spent years photographing bloodstained pavement and broken bodies for the misery-hungry tabloids, seeing in the constant stream of pathos and fright something more than a front-page shot, seeing something tragic and universal which he sought to capture as an artist, so too did Tony Hillerman build up an immense store of such impressions and insights during his many years as a journalist. In fiction, they began to flow forth.

No job exposes a writer more often to that basic raw material of fiction — people under stress. It accumulates: the woman trying to recapture the logic that led her to kill her sleeping husband and her child, the teenaged boy still smelling of smoke who might have saved his brothers from their burning home, but saved himself instead. The oil company executive who has just lost a bankruptcy battle and with it all he has lived for most of his life. The man on death row who believes his mother might claim his body and bury it in some private place, if you could only find her for him. . . . The hungry dream of the anthropology student hoping to prove a thesis in the dust of what was once a Folsom Man hunting camp. The teenaged sisters in the sheriff's office signing the papers which accuse their father of raping them. All handled in five hundred words or less — or maybe a thousand if you have a loose edition. (*Talking Mysteries* 28)

For a journalist who aspires to write something on a grander scale, to write, let's say, a novel, a certain desperation can set in as the days and months and years go by and still the novel has yet to be written. All of those heart-wrenching tales of woe and pain take their toll, and at last many journalists give up their pretensions to imaginative writing, to be replaced by a worldly cynicism and the quasi-proprietorship of a certain stool at a local bar.

The truth which the journalist must constantly face is hazardous in the extreme. Tony Hillerman recognized, when he left the world of newspapers in 1962, that he had come to a turning point. Unlike most journalists, or people, for that matter, he chose the difficult path, and after several transitional years, he was finally ready to truly begin.

Working with facts, as a journalist must, is like working with marble. Truth has its beauty but it doesn't bend. In the seventeen years I spent covering crime and violence, politics, and that "deviation from the normal," which journalism defines as news, the longing grew to take a vacation from the hard rock and move into the plastic of fiction. Instead of spending a laborious week digging out elusive facts, simply make them up. If you want a rumble of thunder outside the courtroom, then thunder rumbles. If you need a one-legged Navajo to make an ironic remark, you create the Navajo, strike off a leg, and he says exactly what you want him to say. (*Talking Mysteries* 28)

As it happened, when Hillerman needed an entire plot, he turned to the Navajo Reservation. Hillerman had for many years been studying Navajo culture and exploring the Navajo Reservation in an enthusiastic if somewhat haphazard way. From the outset he had sensed a certain kinship with the Navajo world, in particular with their balancing of the public and private spheres of life, and their humble yet solemn concern with each individual's place in the cosmos. As the reservation is a mere two-hour drive from Albuquerque, Hillerman had spent many long hours puttering down rutted lanes and walking along the startlingly beautiful mesas with which the Navajo landscape is filled.

One day, as he perused his morning newspaper, a story caught his eye. An Apache policeman had been shot on northern New Mexico's Jicarilla Reservation while trying to capture two men caught stealing gasoline. Though he had been wounded in the arm, and had eventually bled to death, the tribal officer had nonetheless had the physical strength and presence of mind to switch the gun from one hand to the other, and shoot back at his attackers, wounding one. The story stayed with Hillerman, and when it came time to outline his novel, he remembered the Apache policeman. If Joe Leaphorn had a real-life model, then it was that courageous but long-dead Apache.

Hillerman had decided early on in his ponderings that his novel would be set on one of the local reservations. At first, based on that newspaper story, he thought to set it in Apache territory. But he quickly realized that he knew far more about the Navajos, and he moved the locale to the "Big Reservation," the Navajo Reserve, which is the largest in America and which covers twenty-six thousand square miles of arid, sparsely inhabited land. Hillerman was aware that his strength lay in his descriptive abilities, and setting his novel on this magnificently evocative and varied landscape would help him amass the eighty thousand words which he had determined were necessary for a complete novel.

First, originally, I had a long-standing interest in Navajo culture and a love for the landscape, the desert, mountain desert country, dry country, empty country, I liked it. So,

Tony and Lt. Ben Shirley, west of Tuba City.

PHOTO COURTESY TERRENCE MOORE

okay, now I wanted to write a novel. . . . I've a pretty good notion of certain things I'm good at. I'm good at writing narrative action, done it all my life in non-fiction, and I'm good at description. I don't know if I can plot worth a damn, so I said I will set this book in an exotic culture. If the plot's weak, people will be caught up by the culture. Right? That was what I was doing. I wanted an interesting stage setting, to me at least. (Ross and Silet 123)

Despite his yearning to escape the rigid world of facts, Hillerman had spent far too many years working with them, and had far too much respect for the Navajo culture he was intending to describe, to dispense with them entirely. He wanted his book to reflect accurately the culture on the reservation. And inasmuch as his plot would in part deal with Skinwalkers, with the very sensitive issue of Navajo witchcraft, he wanted very much to get his facts right. And yet, he didn't want to write an anthropological treatise either. So he designed a set of rules for himself.

[M]y first priority must be to keep the story moving. [Therefore] . . . any ethnographic material I work in must be germane to the plot. No fair digressing into marriage customs of the Dine', or the way the sexes were separated in the emergence myth, or the penalties for violating the incest taboo, unless it fits. I have no license to teach anthropology. . . . In the second place, the name of the game is telling stories. . . . (*Talking Mysteries* 39)

Although he did not have a licence to teach anthropology, Hillerman nonetheless took his studies of Navajo culture very seriously. He spent many long hours in the UNM Southwest Studies Library, reading treaties and treatises, listening to recorded oral histories and storytellers, and studying the rituals of the Navajo religion. He meandered around the reserve — stopping to talk at trading posts and to stare at unusual rock formations, pausing for the smell of the rain or to watch an eagle hunting or a vulture scavenging — gathering all of the myriad images and sensations which would come to inform his characters' lives.

> When I was writing *Blessing*, I climbed down into the Canyon de Chelly, puddled around on its quicksandy bottom, and collected a headful of sensory impressions (the way the wind sounds down there, the nature of echoes, the smell of sage and wet sand, how the sky looks atop a tunnel of stone, the booming of thunder bouncing from one cliff to another). I seem to write in scenes, and to get the job done I need to remember the details of the stage settings — even though I may use only a few of them. (*Talking Mysteries* 35)

Hillerman began writing his novel in 1967, though he progressed only sporadically, often leaving the pile of typewritten pages untouched for months at a time when his workload was too heavy at UNM, or when his faith in the project deserted him. He began by writing an outline, and then another outline, and then another one. And each time he tried to work out all the complex details of his plot, he ended up utterly baffled and paralyzed by the arcane strategizing. Finally, having decided that his plot might simply evolve if he more or less ignored it, he decided to start writing without one.

However, when Hillerman began writing, spending as much time as he could afford to on several tremendously detailed, ruthlessly crafted first chapters, he found that these too were dead ends. He would rewrite and rewrite those first pages until that first chapter was perfectly honed and trimmed. Unfortunately, he had to toss it, and all subsequent first chapters, away almost as soon as he had finished them. It took Hillerman numerous such attempts before he learned what he calls "The First Chapter Law":

> I suspect I had the first inklings of this law about one hundred pages deep into the first book. By then the anthro-

pologist who was the central character had taken on a distinct personality in my mind. . . . He was not really the sort of fellow I had intended him to be, less heroic and more academic — the product of the author associating with too many live anthropology professors, I suspect. Another character, an officer of the Navajo Tribal Police whom I had intended to be nothing more than a cardboard device for passing along information to the reader, had also taken on three dimensions and was clamoring for a bigger part. Add this to other factors and it was obvious that the wonderful first fourteen pages no longer led into the book I was writing. Out it went, with no more trauma than amputating one's thumb. I wrote a new first chapter which established mood, put the reader into the canyon country, and announced that the game would be Navajo witchcraft. (*Talking Mysteries* 31)

This Navajo tribal policeman to whom Hillerman refers was of course Joe Leaphorn, who made his first appearance in this first Hillerman novel, *The Blessing Way*. Unlike later novels, wherein Hillerman tried to ensure that every detail of Navajo life and culture was accurate, he uncharacteristically and blithely selected an utterly invented and entirely non-Navajo name for his policeman. There are no Navajos named Leaphorn. The name was a sort of poetic amalgam of sounds and meanings drawn from a book Hillerman had been reading at the time — *The Bull from the Sea*, Mary Renault's account of ancient Cretan culture. Leaphorn's evocative surname is perhaps the greatest self-indulgence Hillerman allows himself in the entire range of his Navajo novels. Leaphorn's surname, and, in one sense, his character too. For Leaphorn — a loner who nonetheless understands and has compassion for the labyrinths of human motivation, who is devoted to his wife, is cynical yet highly moral, a Navajo with a university degree whose personal struggles with questions of faith and identity have distanced him from both the Navajo and white worlds — this wily middle-aged man may well, more than any other individual in Hillerman's novels, reflect a conscious or unconscious autobiographical inclination on the author's part.

The Blessing Way was written for Hillerman himself. Although he had always hoped for an audience, and believed that without one creative work was a failure, the writing of this first novel was first and foremost the purging of an old demon for the man who had been imagining doing so for twenty years. The later novels were written with the knowledge that they would be published, that they would have a readership — and that consequently they must above all be stories for the reader. *The Blessing Way* is different. It was a youthful dream realized, and in it we find less of the accomplished fiction-writer-to-be, and more of the man himself, unmasked.

> That short first book required almost three years of spare time. . . . It was also frequently interrupted by moments of sanity. It would occur to me in these periods of lucid reality that no publisher would ever print the stuff I was writing, no one would ever read it, what I was doing was an unconscionable waste of typewriter ribbon. At such times I would put the book on the closet shelf to collect dust until the urge revived itself.
>
> Even at that pace, if the book is short enough you finally finish it. In the case of what came to be *The Blessing Way* this didn't exactly happen. I almost finished it. All that was needed was a final chapter in which justice was done and all questions resolved in an ultimate flurry of exciting action. This eluded me. Finally, sick of the entire project, I tacked on an ending in which the bad guy is shot. I sent it off to my agent. (*Talking Mysteries* 31–32)

Hillerman's agent was Ann Elmo, whose New York agency had placed numerous articles for Hillerman. These articles were those written for his master's thesis and included the detective piece on the bubonic plague for *True* magazine. When Hillerman announced to his agent his intention to write a novel, she suggested that journalists should stick to journalism and not experiment with entirely different kinds of writing which she would not be able to sell and which would make both of them look bad. It was not a vote of confidence, but neither was it unreasonable advice. Yet, as artists will, Hillerman happily ignored her advice and instead, some years later, sent her a manuscript.

The judgement was pointed and severe: the book was awful; the Indian stuff was corny; if he insisted on trying to publish the book, then he would have to cut out all the Indian stuff and stick to blood-and-guts thriller action. Hillerman was daunted but not convinced. He had recently come across an article by Joan Kahn, the mystery editor for Harper and Row, who had spoken about the plasticity and breadth of possibility within the mystery genre. Perhaps she would understand.

Thus Hillerman sent that initial fateful letter asking Kahn to decide whether author or agent had more accurately assessed this particular manuscript. Her acceptance of the role of arbiter was immediate. Hillerman's response was equally swift, as he mailed off the manuscript upon receiving her reply. Ten days later Hillerman set out to attend a conference in New York City. He called Joan Kahn on the off chance that she might have read the book. Her reply: "Haven't you received my letter? We want to publish it."

7

First it was "Enemy Way." Then "Monsterslayer." Finally Harper and Row decided this first mystery novel by an unknown author should be titled *The Blessing Way*. Hillerman agreed, although the key curing ceremony in the novel is in fact an Enemy Way and not a Blessing Way. Twenty-five years earlier, the youthful Hillerman had attended an Enemy Way ceremony during his first visit to the reservation, and his memories of that initial experience informed his new book. Though changing the title was a compromise, it was a minor one, and in any event Hillerman was in no position to argue the point. Years later he remarked that the pious-sounding title still lured the occasional Christian book-buyer to purchase the novel under the mistaken impression that it would offer them spiritual guidance.

At the time of publication, in early 1970, nobody could have foreseen that Tony Hillerman would eventually become one of the best-selling mystery authors in America. Hillerman himself, it is worth recalling, had only imagined the writing of *The Blessing Way* as a tune-up for his real novel. Yet, in retrospect, in rereading the first "Hillerman," virtually all of the major themes that now characterize the series can be discerned in the first few pages of *The Blessing Way*.

Take, for example, the very first paragraph of the book, in which Luis Horseman carefully sets a series of deadfalls to trap kangaroo rats. Already in these first few lines we are drawn in by Hillerman's use of words and names which are unfamiliar to most readers. Kangaroo rats, piñon twigs, deadfalls — these are hardly the standard accoutrements of detective fiction. Luis Horseman takes care in setting his precisely balanced trap. He then rocks back on his heels and begins to sing a hunting song to the animals. Here, the fragile and precarious nature of human existence is emphasized, a theme which Hillerman will return to again and again. Nature is to be treated with respect because it is more powerful than we are. Supplication may achieve a sort of harmony with nature but there are no guarantees. In fact, when Horseman finishes his song, his first thought is that he isn't singing the song properly and doesn't know how the rest goes. This uncertainty too is indicative of the central drama of Hillerman's future novels.

Faith is the preeminent Hillerman theme. His characters struggle with moral dilemmas which lead them to question their faith: faith in human justice, in divine justice, in the justice of nature or the lack thereof; the difficulty of maintaining faith in the face of evil, in the face of mortality and suffering; faith in traditions, in the way of one's ancestors; faith in medicine, in the healing power of community, in oneself. These are the essential challenges which Joe Leaphorn and Jim Chee constantly face. The murder plots that they untangle, while offering the skeleton of a story, are ultimately nothing more than platforms upon which the eminently reasonable and highly active consciences of Leaphorn and Chee can play out their struggles with faith.

One of the most captivating scenes in The Blessing Way, and perhaps the very best writing in the novel, occurs when Joe Leaphorn attends an Enemy Way ceremony dressed in jeans to search for information regarding the inexplicable murder of Luis Horseman. Leaphorn believes that the Singer who is conducting the ritual may have some knowledge of Horseman's killing. Perhaps, Leaphorn wonders, it is even Horseman who is being symbolically killed by the ritual. Leaphorn questions the elder, whose name is Sandoval, with a subtlety and ease which pleases the old man.

> "My grandfather, I hope all is well with you," his voice is very clear and distinct. Sandoval, who had noticed lately that most young people mumbled, liked this. He invited the young man to sit beside him.

"I am called Joe Leaphorn," the young man said, "and I work for Law and Order," but after that he talked about other things — about the rains starting early this year, which was good, and about drinking and gambling at the ceremonials, which was bad. Sandoval approved of this, knowing that the policeman would get around to his business in good time and appreciating that here was a young one who knew the old and patient ways. (94)

Their conversation continues for several pages, each sparring gently with the other, playing an age-old game of wit-matching until Leaphorn has learned all he can. Then, as they rise to leave, it is the Singer's turn to ask a question. "Tell me if you believe in witching," Sandoval says. Leaphorn replies expansively that he has learned about witchcraft from his father, who taught him the origin myths and the nature of witchcraft. "You didn't tell me whether you believe it," Sandoval correctly replies. "My grandfather," Leaphorn finally answers, "I have learned to believe in evil."

Here we find the philosophical core of all Hillerman novels: the struggle of faith versus evil. Each in his own way, Leaphorn and Chee struggle with this issue from one mystery to the next. Leaphorn believes in evil. He does not believe in witchcraft. Yet he can never fully acknowledge the implications of this choice. He clings to his faith in the orderliness of nature, in the value of the old ways, even when he recognizes his distance from them. Chee, when he eventually arrives on the scene, will deal with this problem differently. He attempts to use his will to overcome the seemingly unavoidable conflict between the moral realms of the police officer and the medicine man. His success is never assured, and his faith in his double life is constantly under assault. It is these twin struggles — mirroring the struggles that each of us, in our own way, are forced to engage in — that make Hillerman's novels so compelling. As in all great genre writing, whether it be detective fiction, science fiction, travel writing, or any other kind, the story in *The Blessing Way* is merely a vehicle for the exploration of the internal dramas of the human psyche.

In choosing certain elements with which to introduce the reader to his story in the opening pages of *The Blessing Way*, Hillerman also chose, unbeknownst to himself, the very elements which would prove to be his central tools and literary interests in the years to come. On page 3, Luis Horseman stands up and then looks "carefully across the plateau, searching the foreground first, then the mid-distance, finally the great green slopes of the Lukachukai Mountains, which rose to the east." Horseman is just the first of many characters who will look into the distance in the thousands of pages to come. Tony Hillerman is enamoured of distance, of the dimensions of physical space and the implications for the human landscape. Hillerman loves the way clouds, mountains, mesas, and valleys emphasize and amplify the geography of the human mind. Time and again Leaphorn and Chee will stand and gaze off into the distance, allowing their thoughts to merge with the surrounding natural patterns and thereby gain coherency and shape.

This fascination with distance is inextricably bound up with the natural landscape of the Navajo Reservation itself. This is a land characterized by space. In land such as Hillerman describes, the microcosm is never too far away from the macrocosm. All one need do is step outside to be surrounded by uncounted miles of emptiness above and on all sides; or to be impaled by the enormity of a five-hundred-foot-high block of rock sitting alone in one's front yard; or hurled back through centuries by any of the thousands of Anasazi sites dotting the Four Corners region. Just as the Himalayas, with their inescapable grandeur, could not be other than a spiritual realm, so does the land of the Navajo require a spiritual commitment. Hillerman makes that commitment so passionately, and translates his faith in the land with such fervour and grace, that he successfully converts his readers to that same faith. We have all of us canyons and deserts in our minds, dim genetic memories of wandering and of awe before the immensity of nature. It is that deeply rooted collective memory which Hillerman awakes with his natural descriptions.

Jim Peshlakai and Tony at Coalmine Mesa.

The Blessing Way offers one last marvellous indication of Hillerman's method: his pacing. On several occasions we spend long pages accompanying a minor character engaged in a time-consuming task. Hillerman doesn't stint here. In chapter 5, for example, we meet a character named Joseph Begay, who has no other role in the novel than finding Luis Horseman's body as he drives into town to pick up his daughter at the bus station. Yet Begay, whose life and actions are of no direct relevance whatsoever to the plot, is nonetheless introduced to us some five pages before he finds the body, as he wakes to a beautiful morning sunrise. We witness his awakening, his smelling of "the rain smells, dampened dust, wet sage, piñon resin and buffalo grass" (40). We are present as he thinks back to when he first built his hogan, and why he built it where he did, and how he built it; and we watch him rise and go outside to make breakfast and examine the weather. Finally, he gets into his truck and heads toward town, singing to himself. But still, he must travel two more pages, up and down Teastah Wash, before at last he fulfils his role in the story and finds the body of Luis Horseman.

Why has Hillerman included all this apparently irrelevant material? Obviously, because it is not irrelevant to him. Joseph Begay is a part of the harmony of the story. This is not a whodunit where a body appears by the side of the road with a sign on it saying "Clue #2." On the contrary, Hillerman is telling us that his story is really about people like Joseph Begay, about real life, normal everyday life, in which a dead body by the roadside is utterly incongruous. And what is more, the dead body is probably less important, in the long run, and most certainly to Joseph Begay, than making sure he is there to pick up his daughter on time.

In life, things take time. Other novelists might gloss over the irrelevancies, the unimportant moments, the song a minor character happens to be singing when he or she enters the drama. Hillerman does not. To him, these moments are necessary. Without them there could be no sense of the time it takes for events to occur, for clouds to travel across the horizon, for a curing ceremony to happen. Inner struggles endure, like days, like seasons, like lives. There is no sense in camouflaging the distance between events and people. In the way he chooses to pace his stories, by offering us an extended glimpse into the life of Joseph Begay, or seven pages describing the Enemy Way ceremony in human detail — the faces, the smells, the activities, the concerns, the tiredness, the rambunctiousness, the dreaminess of it all — Hillerman requests, and generally receives, our entrance into his world. True, it is a world filled with unfamiliar sights, smells, and sounds, but it is also a world concerned with the time it takes to cook a meal, or to get dressed, or to drive two hundred miles, and these are familiar indeed. This emphasizing of familiar details is an old storytelling technique which links the reader to the otherwise foreign places and people, and it is one which Hillerman employs beautifully.

But how does *The Blessing Way* stand up to critical examination as a complete work, and in comparison with Hillerman's later efforts? The answer seems to be that it is an excellent first try, but the book is nonetheless seriously flawed. Hillerman himself has said that his reputation as an author would probably be far better had the novel not been published. The underlying problem with *The Blessing Way* is that the author was not aware of the true subject of his book until it was too late to do anything about it.

While he was writing it, Hillerman thought that *The Blessing Way* was about Bergen McKee, an anthropologist from UNM, and Ellen Leon, McKee's eventual love interest. Yet in the end, neither of these two characters is remotely believable. McKee is a cardboard hero, while Leon is simply cardboard, offering no hint of any depth of character. Hillerman is too caught up in trying to create characters that fulfil Creative Writing 301 requirements for "character drawing." Only when his Navajo characters appear — Leaphorn, Horseman, Sandoval, Begay — does Hillerman's story come to life. Not because the Indians give stereotyped colour to the story, but because his Navajo characters are clearly defined and richly detailed. Their motivations, idiosyncracies, and actions are all eminently coherent and fluid. By

comparison, McKee's woodenness is reminiscent of a mario-
nette, with the puppeteer's hands not quite hidden behind a
curtain.

Hillerman's apparent success when characterizing Navajos,
and lack thereof when describing whites, raises an interesting
question. Might it be that his characterizations of Navajos are
equally unrealistic but that white readers are unable to recognize
this because of their ignorance with regard to Navajo culture
and life?

There are two ways of answering this question. The first is
Hillerman's own response: We are all the same under the skin,
and it is only natural that he should be able to describe Leaphorn
more accurately than McKee because he understands people
like Leaphorn far better than he has ever understood people like
McKee. The second, somewhat more objective, method of
determining the validity of Hillerman's characterizations of
Navajos is to examine the response of the Navajos themselves.
And here Hillerman is clearly on solid ground. For, over the
years, he has received so much fan mail from Navajos, been
invited to so many Navajo events, spent so much time on the
reservation talking to individual Navajos, that any doubts about
the popularity of his books among the Navajo can be erased. In
fact, before Hillerman became a national figure whose books
sold in stores around the world, he was an important local hero
whose dog-eared books were passed from hand to hand on the
reservation, from one Navajo family to another. The inhabitants
of the reservations were Hillerman's first fans.

When Hillerman was notified that his manuscript was to be
published, he found his perception of what he had written
changing dramatically.

The MS was no longer merely a box full of typed-upon paper.
It was an incipient BOOK. Everything was suddenly easier.
Gone was the notion that this was wasted time, that I was
only indulging myself. Someone out there was going to
receive the message I was encoding. I found myself back in

the familiar, comfortable world of the professional writer. I had in my hands a thousand-word analysis from a famous editor, full of shrewd questions and suggestions. (*Talking Mysteries* 33)

Hillerman jumped to the task of reworking the manuscript into the form Joan Kahn had asked for. This meant, as Hillerman himself might have predicted, completely rewriting the ending, which had been so nonchalantly tacked on. It also meant, to his pleasure, emphasizing the Navajo setting and culture even more than he had done originally. As it turned out, the more he revised, the more he found one of his characters growing larger and larger.

Leaphorn came into being more or less accidentally in *The Blessing Way* in which, as I had originally intended to write it, he had a very minor role, a *very* minor role in the first draft. When I revised the manuscript knowing it was going to be published, it was all of a sudden very serious, and it was my first book. By then I'd sort of fallen for the guy, so when I revised it into a finished draft for Harper and Row, I beefed up his role and gave him a more substantial part in it, but he was still accidental. . . . (Ross and Silet 120)

A second aspect of *The Blessing Way* that required reworking was Hillerman's use of Navajo ritual poetry. The several poetic verses scattered throughout the text are among the most unusual aspects of the novel, and among the most effective means of slowing the reader down to the real-time pace of Navajo life and ceremony. Concerned about possible copyright infringements, Harper and Row asked Hillerman to identify the sources of his quotations, which, after some research, he was able to do. One passage had been taken from *The Agricultural and Hunting Methods of the Navajo People*, written by a friend and UNM colleague of Hillerman's, W.W. Hill. Another had been taken from a century-old report to the Smithsonian's Bureau of Ethnology.

But, as Hillerman reported in a letter to Kahn's secretary, the verses with which the book more or less begins were untraceable.

> Unfortunately, I couldn't find the source of the stuff in the first chapter. . . . I worked with about 25 books, ethnology reports and so forth and not all of them are currently available to me. . . . Therefore, I rewrote the passages in question, retaining only the tone and the sound. (Letter to Mary McGinn, 1 Aug. 1969)

In an earlier letter, Hillerman had explained his approach to these ritual poems:

> The problem of copyrights and permissions occurred to me while I was writing THE BLESSING WAY and I believe I handled it so as to avoid this trouble. Let me explain.
>
> The Navajos haven't had a written language very long and it isn't used very widely. Their ritual poetry has been handed down in the oral tradition. It tends, thus, to vary between parts of the reservation and between individual Singers, Hand-tremblers and so forth. And it also tends to vary between books.
>
> To avoid infringing on anyone's copyright, I sort of made up my own poetry, trying to retain the authentic pattern of sounds to make it sound genuine to the reader but mixing it up enough and rewording it so that it is really nothing more than a synthetic Hillerman version of Navajo chants. (Letter to Mary McGinn, 28 July 1969)

At last, by February 1970, *The Blessing Way* was printed and ready to be released. Hillerman flew to New York for the publication party, and with best-of-lucks ringing in his ears, *The Blessing Way* was distributed to stores and placed on the market.

The results at first were less than overwhelming. Nobody declared Hillerman the heir apparent to Ross Macdonald or

Raymond Chandler. *The Blessing Way* was not a best-seller, nor anything remotely like one. And yet, there were a number of encouraging signs. The book was, for example, nominated for the Best First Mystery Novel Edgar Award by the Mystery Writers of America. It eventually lost out to *The Anderson Tapes* by Lawrence Sanders, but it was awarded an Honourable Mention. Of far more significance, at least from the perspective of the book's publisher, was the American Library Association's listing of *The Blessing Way* as one of the year's "Notable Books." Inclusion on the ALA list meant that the book was certain now to remain in print for a long time, and for a publisher, this counted for more than any awards or honourable mentions.

This was one of the most active periods in Tony Hillerman's consistently active life. He was teaching journalism at UNM and was chair of his department. He was working on several other books (*The Boy Who Made Dragonfly*, a children's book illustrated by his daughter Janet, and *The Great Taos Bank Robbery*, a collection of the articles he had written for his master's thesis), writing magazine articles, and being a father to his six children. At the age of forty-four, Hillerman had successfully begun his third career. And to his amazement, this one would make Tony Hillerman one of the most popular storytellers in America.

8

Having published a novel, Tony Hillerman could now legitimately regard himself as a novelist, a genuine fiction writer, a former journalist successfully reborn as an author. And now that he was an author, the time had come to write his Great American Novel, his *War and Peace*. Hillerman had often used these terms, half-mockingly, when describing the novel he had long dreamed of writing. It was not a Navajo novel but something much closer to his heart, to his experience, to his life. It would be a novel about a political reporter in a state capital. In fact, it would be an only semi-imaginary autobiography.

The result was *The Fly on the Wall* (1971), a terrific thriller which resonates with descriptive accuracy and narrative authenticity. Unlike *The Blessing Way*'s Bergen McKee, this second book's protagonist, ace reporter John Cotton, is utterly believable. Equally believable are the secondary characters, the political intrigue, the physical descriptions, and the investigative procedures — it all rings perfectly, seamlessly true. What is more remarkable, however, is that having finally written the book that had lain so close to his heart for so many years, Tony Hillerman abandoned its universe entirely and remained thereafter committed exclusively to the adventures of Joe Leaphorn and Jim Chee.

Why? Why was Joseph Cotton not turned into a recurring hero instead of Joe Leaphorn? Why had Hillerman's years of experience as a political reporter suddenly grown stale? Why didn't this ex-journalist write more journalistic mysteries?

The answers appear to be several. First, Hillerman had placed such high expectations upon this particular book that it was virtually inevitable that the result should fail to live up to his dreams. Furthermore, in writing *The Blessing Way*, Hillerman had enjoyed the freedom that storytelling affords, the freedom to invent, to superimpose, to recreate. Suddenly, in attempting to not simply tell a story, but to gather all of his past into a coherent whole, to give meaning to those fifteen years as a reporter, to confront the moral questions that had plagued him for so long, suddenly the imagination seemed less free. In fact, he felt bound.

> Unlike *The Blessing Way*, or any of the books I've finished since, I had a pretty fair grasp of the plot of this one before I started — or at least I thought I did. But when I got into it, I found my storytelling instincts at war with my urge to give the reader a truly realistic view of the professional life of a political reporter. . . . To keep the narrative moving, I had to cut out the details needed to give it that DEEPER MEANING that writers talk about after they anoint themselves with the sacred oil of art. (*Talking Mysteries* 34)

In Hillerman's case, that deeper meaning, as always in his stories, meant struggling with the essentially moral paradox all journalists must face: the deeper into the story one delves, the more emotionally bound to its resolution one becomes, and yet the more neutral and impartial one is required to be. Despite his trivializing of artistic intentions, Hillerman was deeply concerned that these issues be given the scope and importance he felt they deserved. In *The Fly on the Wall*, Hillerman identifies three methods of coping with this paradox, all of which he had encountered time and again as a journalist and editor. The first is cynicism, the second is egotism, and the third is escapism.

One of the novel's most revealing lines occurs early on, when John Cotton, capitol reporter in an unnamed midwestern state, notices that a coworker, Merrill McDaniels, "had been excited, which was surprising. No one in the pressroom was ever excited" (6). Cynical. Jaded. Blasé. Unfazed. These are all apt descriptions of the journalist's usual refuge from the trauma of witnessing, day after day, the slings and arrows of outrageous fortune which have been visited upon the local citizenry. Hillerman himself, when he left the Santa Fe *New Mexican*, did so largely to avoid falling victim to the lifelessness that can overtake a journalist who has seen too much of life yet felt too little, a toll he had seen exacted from his peers.

The second kind of journalist in Hillerman's novel is the egotistical journalist: one who takes his or her position of power as an end in and of itself, who feels that because journalists are privileged to meet with, socialize with, and report on the activities of the powerful, they too must be of great worth. Often these journalists end up, as do several of John Cotton's colleagues, working at impressive salaries for not-so-impressive politicians. Or, like Cotton's respected elder in the capitol building's pressroom, Leroy Hall, they serve a good cause but with an exaggerated sense of their own importance:

> "We buy this business of give them the facts and man decides in his enlightened self-interest. How about changing it — being realistic? Deciding that sometimes they're not going to digest the facts and come to the enlightened conclusion. You know it's true. You've seen it time after time." Hall looked up, his eyes on Cotton's eyes. "How about making a selection sometimes of what facts they can handle — giving them what's good for them?"
> "You feel like playing God?" Cotton laughed. "I'm not ready for it." (83–84)

Here we find encapsulated the argument that each conscientious reporter must have with himself every day, if he is not to fall into the trap of either completely believing himself or completely disbelieving others. And yet, maintaining a balance is difficult. Halfway through *The Fly on the Wall*, John Cotton thinks about quitting his job. He has met a woman who thinks he is heartless and mean for exposing the petty deceits of bureaucrats. Cotton realizes, by the book's end, that neither side is right. That neither his editor, nor the police, nor the politicians, nor anybody else truly knows the answers. Sure, each knows that certain causes will produce certain effects, but who knows what it all means? Who ultimately benefits? Who gets hurt? Abandoning his attempt to make sense of it, Cotton decides to quit. He gets the story out, but he is through with journalism — for the moment anyway. As it turns out, now that he has finally proven both to himself and to the woman he loves that he does care, that he cares enough to run away from it, he decides to stay, and to reenter the fray. This time, however, knowing now that he can no longer be neutral, Cotton — like his friend Leroy Hall whom he had never understood — will play God. He *will* care what happens and will try to affect the outcome accordingly. He will be a lesser journalist but a better person.

The story is gripping and realistic. Journalists must make these choices. Yet, if we compare Cotton's decision to Hillerman's, there is a distinct contrast. Hillerman struggled for years with the same issues as Cotton, yet eventually he opted out. He took his conscience off the fire and began to let the years of built-up steam emerge in stories, in imaginary tales, in novels like *The Fly on the Wall*. And though we are speaking here of a novel, and of an imaginary character, there can be no doubt that in many ways John Cotton, like Joe Leaphorn, *is* Tony Hillerman.

For example, Cotton and Hillerman favour the same card games: poker and a solitaire game called Spider, which Hillerman likes to play for hours at a time. They both love fishing, and when Cotton goes fishing in the Brazos, it is to a spot described by Hillerman years later in his travel book, *Hillerman Country*, as a place he has been fishing for years. Cotton's big story concerns the machinations of a corrupt gang of highway officials involved in a contracting scam. Strangely enough, Hillerman broke just such a story during his days as state capitol reporter in Oklahoma. Cotton even mentions an incident that occurred in Borger, Texas, an obscure west Texas town where Tony Hillerman just happened to have served as a police reporter some twenty-odd years before *The Fly on the Wall* was written.

PHOTO COURTESY CENTER FOR SOUTHWEST RESEARCH

NO. 000-501-0002

I wrote it from the single viewpoint of John Cotton, an introverted political reporter. I was totally comfortable in John Cotton's mind, prowling a state capitol as familiar as the palm of my hand and dealing with people I know as well as my own family. . . . [T]he investigative techniques used by Cotton are simply a description of techniques I had used to dig through records. . . . Yet comfortable as I was with Cotton, even before I finished that book I was yearning to get back to the Navajo Reservation and back to Navajo Tribal Policeman Joe Leaphorn. (*Talking Mysteries* 34–35)

It seems likely that Hillerman, despite having looked forward for years to writing this book, found the subject matter too close to home, too difficult to step outside of and assess. He was able to accurately describe a long list of minor characters and dramatic incidents, as well as the workings of a complex and determined protagonist, yet the fictional choices made by John Cotton had been made by the real-life Hillerman years earlier, and they had resulted in a different ending than the one played out in the book.

In real life, Hillerman gave up investigative journalism. He stopped trying to play God in a world in which there was too much competition with other would-be deities — the rich, the powerful, and the righteous. Instead, he took up a different kind of writing, one in which he could play God without any rivals, in which he could create his own worlds, in which the meaning he so anxiously sought could actually be found. Not, as he discovered in *The Fly on the Wall*, in grandiose ambitions and lofty justifications, but as his "storytelling instinct" repeatedly informed him, in stories of nature, of belief, of washing and drying, of eating and sleeping, and even — to keep the reader quite satisfied — of the occasional corpse.

"I will always have ambiguous feelings about *Fly*," Hillerman admits. "It fell far short of what I had intended. And, despite generally good reviews, it didn't sell well. But it is still a favorite" (*Talking Mysteries* 34). Later, asked by an interviewer why he had not followed up with more journalistic mysteries, Hillerman replies,

I kind of don't know why myself. That's what I'd been, and obviously I've never been a Navajo and it was relatively easy to write *Fly* because it was all right out of memory, just move things around. But I don't know. Before I was finished with it, I had a feeling I wanted to hurry up and get this damn thing done and get back and do the Navajo thing better. (Ross and Silet 125)

9

Having published his somewhat disappointing masterpiece, Hillerman eagerly returned to Joe Leaphorn and the Navajo Reservation. He had been dissatisfied with numerous aspects of *The Blessing Way*, and in his next novel, which would be unmistakably a Joe Leaphorn novel, he would try to make amends. The result was *Dance Hall of the Dead* (1973), an unprecedented American suspense thriller about a series of murders on the Hopi Reservation. A Navajo boy is implicated in the killings, thus requiring Joe Leaphorn's intervention.

Dance Hall of the Dead, Hillerman's second Navajo novel, won the Edgar Allan Poe Award for Best Mystery of the Year from the Mystery Writers of America. This confirmed what had already become apparent: Tony Hillerman was not only able to write fiction, but he was also extremely good at it. Interestingly, in a handwritten notebook filled with notes and bits of chapters from *Dance Hall of the Dead*, Hillerman wrote a manifesto to himself, one that summarizes the approach to writing which led to his success. It begins with the headline "Platitudes Truisms and Prejudices":

> [I]t is said that the writer writes only for himself —
> except in a very special sense —
> this is utter nonsense, but it infects a lot of young writers —
> the young because if they don't overcome the infection
> they're not writers very long
> you write for the reader —
> perhaps a single generalized reader —
> of your imagination, perhaps for a single specific person —
> perhaps for a like minded group —

perhaps even for followers of the Enemy Gods —
But you *have to write* for someone —
otherwise you're like a man at a telegraph key talking into
a vacuum.
It's totally sterile and self-defeating.
The name of the game is communicating —
sending and receiving —
translating the image inside your skull into symbols and
launching it at a target. If it misses —
if it doesn't produce the same image inside his skull —
then you've failed

(Notebook, Hillerman Collection, UNM)

The messages in *Dance Hall of the Dead* are communicated with clarity and precision, with an overall effectiveness that far surpasses *The Blessing Way*. Leaphorn's character has grown and is beginning to approach the stern but sympathetic Navajo cop that Hillerman's readers would eventually come to know so well. Though the patterns that characterize Hillerman's novels — the transitions from the natural world to the internal psyche, the dry Navajo humour, the emphasis upon dialogue — had their genesis in *The Blessing Way*, they are fully developed in *Dance Hall of the Dead*.

Hillerman has vastly improved his plotting in this second Navajo novel, although once again a pair of white anthropologists are central characters. However, instead of stumbling into a completely unrelated and superimposed series of events, as in *The Blessing Way*, these anthropologists, in a hidden way, *create* the action. Furthermore, while field-worker Ted Isaacs and his psychotically ambitious mentor Dr. Reynolds are essential to the plot, they also cast into relief Navajo customs and beliefs. As the Navajo world grows clearer and more distinct, the white world grows ever more confusing, less decipherable, less stable. The world of white science and facts is obscured by the spiritual dynamic which steers Leaphorn's search for the young Navajo mystic, George Bowlegs. This process is one that satisfies both Hillerman's Navajo readers, who welcome a realistic presentation of Navajo morality, and his white readers, many of whom already feel alienated from materialistic values and welcome the appearance of an alternative moral model.

When Leaphorn confronts the innocent dupe Ted Isaacs with evidence that his boss had been planting prehistoric flint in the site Isaacs was working, and had then killed three people to cover up his fraud, the Navajo policeman can barely restrain his contempt for white values, for the values that would lead a man to kill a boy to protect his reputation. In offering Isaacs a simple way out of the mess, offering him essentially the enticing fruits of another man's demented actions, Leaphorn chides Isaacs:

> "Come on," Leaphorn said. "Can't you understand what I'm saying?" His voice was angry. . . . "I'm saying," Leaphorn gritted through his teeth, "just how much do you want fame and fortune and a faculty job? A couple of days ago you wanted it worse than you wanted that girl of yours. How about now? You want it bad enough to lie a little?" (165)

Leaphorn, who is usually a kindly if somewhat gruff man, is also at times extremely bitter in this novel. His descriptions of Kit Carson's pillaging and murdering of Navajos, and his memory of his Bureau of Indian Affairs high school, which sought to destroy the old beliefs, add to Leaphorn's character an intriguing reservoir of tension and realism. So does Hillerman's casual intra-tribal police banter. In one scene, Leaphorn tries to sort out jurisdictions with the Zuñi policeman Ed Pasquaanti and the FBI. After the departure of the handsomely inept FBI agent John O'Malley, who unintentionally patronizes these men with one stereotypical comment after another, they share a joke:

> "It's like my daddy always told me," Pasquaanti said. "Never trust no goddamn Induns. That right, Lieutenant?"
> "That's right," Leaphorn said. "My grandmother had a

motto hanging there in the hogan when I was a kid. Said 'Beware All Blanket-Asses.' " (71)

Through humour, Hillerman attains a degree of humanism and understanding that deepens the reader's appreciation of difference. Just as Leaphorn and Pasquaanti, traditional antagonists as Navajo and Zuñi, manage, through such banter, to come to an understanding of what they share, as well as how they differ, Hillerman aims to develop a similar understanding in his white readers with respect to Navajos in particular, and native people in general.

The white characters in *Dance Hall of the Dead* are far more complex and far more believable than the distressingly two-dimensional white protagonists in *The Blessing Way*. Hillerman's descriptions of the hippie commune cum heroin-smuggling operation include a number of startlingly real encounters. The wayward teenage girl, Susanne, who has gotten mixed up with this crowd, is beautifully drawn. Her self-doubt, her compassion, her intelligence, fear, and courage — these qualities are only hinted at in Leaphorn's conversations with her, but through his sympathetic eyes we see an all-too-familiar figure. Leaphorn tries to help her, and may or may not have succeeded as the book ends. This ambiguity too is part of Hillerman's refreshing realism.

And finally, there is George Bowlegs himself, the fourteen-year-old boy who is accused of murdering Ernesto Cata and who is himself murdered in the book's compelling climax. Hillerman might have let the boy live. There is no reason, in terms of solving the crime, that the boy has to die. Yet, for spiritual reasons, inasmuch as Bowlegs has broken a Zuñi taboo, he has to meet his fate. Despite his best attempts, Leaphorn, who has chased the boy throughout the novel, is unable to save him, and the boy dies in his arms.

When *Dance Hall of the Dead* was optioned as a potential film, and then as a television series, the first thing Hillerman was told was that Bowlegs couldn't be killed off at the end. No audience would be able to handle that sort of depressing ending.

Dance Hall of the Dead has been optioned more than once. I've got a file in my office labeled KEEPING GEORGE BOWLEGS ALIVE. Twice now producers have brought him back from the dead. I didn't realize he'd been resurrected for the first time because I didn't read their script for a number of years. . . . Then Bob Banner, a television producer who's a real old pro and whom I admire greatly, thought we could sell Warner Bros. the idea of making a pilot based on *Dance Hall*. (qtd. in Carr 9)

Unfortunately, when Warner Brothers did assign someone to work with Hillerman to develop the idea, they insisted that the series take place in an urban setting, with reusable characters, no archaeologists, and a number of other criteria transforming Leaphorn into a sort of Navajo Bruce Willis. Needless to say, the idea stalled. Years later, in 1989, Hillerman wrote to a class of Zuñi grade four students, asking them whether *they* thought George Bowlegs should remain alive at the end of the story. To his relief, there was more or less unanimous agreement that it would be unrealistic if Bowlegs survived. Hillerman felt vindicated.

Between the publishing of *Dance Hall of the Dead* (1973) and the next Leaphorn novel, *Listening Woman* (1978), there occurred several events which seriously imperilled Leaphorn's survival. Prominent among these was Hillerman's conflict with the producer Bob Banner, concerning the ownership of the rights to Leaphorn's character. Hillerman suddenly found that, as the result of an apparent misunderstanding, Banner had obtained exclusive ownership of certain rights to Leaphorn. He was worried and upset.

In a letter to Joan Kahn, written just months before *Listening Woman* was published, Hillerman wrote,

It may become important to me to stop using Lt. Joseph Leaphorn and use instead Corporal Charles Begay, another Navajo cop, who is younger, single, more inclined to irreverence, etc. In fact, if I can't get this straightened out . . .

what would you think about me making the switch of characters in *Listening Woman?* . . . Frankly Leaphorn has a bit too much rank for my liking, and his name wasn't as well chosen as it would have been had I known that I was going to be using him more. (20 Sept. 1977)

Eventually, however, the conflict was ironed out, though it did require a sacrifice on Hillerman's part. He had to spend $21,000 to buy back the rights to Leaphorn — or, as he put it in a subsequent interview, "to ransom Joe 'out of slavery.' " "The same month the Ayatollah took the hostages, Bob Banner took Joe Leaphorn" (Breslin 58).

Yet it was more than this conflict which had caused the gap between Leaphorn books. Hillerman had been very busy in the years leading up to *Listening Woman*. He had resigned from the chairmanship of the Journalism Department in 1974, but nonetheless remained on faculty teaching full time. Furthermore, in 1976 he was hired by UNM's new president, William Davis, in a similar capacity to that in which he had served Tom Popejoy, UNM's earlier president. Davis's announcement of the appointment described the job as follows:

As assistant to the president, Professor Hillerman's duties will be of a general administrative nature. . . . He will be involved generally with seeing that policy decisions are carried out and such other responsibilities as may be assigned from time to time. Also he will serve as a direct liaison of my office on general and specific assignments. (qtd. in "Hillerman Winner of Press Award")

Hillerman's appointment was for three years, but he ended up staying five, leaving in 1981 only after a basketball recruitment scandal known as Lobogate had caused enormous damage to the reputation of the school. Although Hillerman was not implicated in the illegal payments to potential recruits, his position as assistant to the president meant he was required to cope with at

PHOTO COURTESY TERRENCE MOORE

least part of the substantial fallout from the scandal. Later he said of that position and those years, "A lot of that was no fun, but you felt that it had to be done. And I really admired the man. I still do" (qtd. in Black B1).

In addition to his university career and his career as a novelist, Hillerman also continued to write nonfiction. Although he still wrote the occasional article for *New Mexico Magazine*, *Arizona Highways*, or Fodor's travel guides, Hillerman had turned his attention to writing for books. In 1974 he published *New Mexico*, which combined photographs by David Muench with a descriptive essay by Hillerman. This was followed a year later by *Rio Grande*, a similar photo-essay with text, this time with photos by Robert Reynolds. In 1976, Hillerman edited a book titled *The Spell of New Mexico*, featuring articles by several well-known New Mexico writers. In that same year, Hillerman was awarded the Dan Burrows Memorial Award for his continuing outstanding contributions to journalism in New Mexico. Thus it is hardly surprising that fans of his Navajo mysteries were forced to wait nearly five years for the appearance of the third book in the series. They would never need wait that long again.

Listening Woman is among the very best writing Hillerman has done. The book is superior to its predecessors in every way, and marks a high point in Hillerman's fiction, and certainly in Leaphorn's career. The Navajo detective is smart, tenacious, gutsy, cynical, and proud. He gets hit by a car, burnt in a fire, attacked by a dog, shot at, nearly suffocated, and yet he endures. He is consumed by a desire to kill a man, and that desire saves him from being consumed by the flames with which his opponent has engulfed him. These are deliciously raw moments, harsher than almost anything that would come in later books. Here, Hillerman has mastered Leaphorn, and mastered his own initial style. Leaphorn as yet has no rivals. He has no wife. Neither Chee nor Emma has yet appeared on Hillerman's dramatis personae. Leaphorn is all alone with a crazed Navajo enemy, and the result is tremendous.

The novel's power is established in the wonderfully conceived opening dichotomy. At first we encounter Listening Woman trying to solve the mystery of Hosteen Tso's spiritual sickness, aided by her niece Anna Atcitty. When Listening Woman leaves and enters her diagnostic trance, Anna and Tso are killed by an unknown stranger. The rest of the book concerns these intricately connected mysteries: on one hand, the spiritual question as to what had so wounded the spirit of Hosteen Tso, and on the other, the material question of who had smashed his body. As the story unfolds, we discover a similar duality in the characters of Hosteen Tso's grandsons, one of whom is a Catholic priest, and the other a murderous native-rights revolutionary. In the end they both die, they both sacrifice themselves for their respective causes, and they do so in the secret, sacred place which had caused Hosteen Tso so much anguish. Neither grandson is redeemed. Both perish, and, we conclude, both perish in the service of fruitless causes. Certainly the priest was less evil, but in the end, perhaps, no less misguided.

Listening Woman is also notable for the introduction of two subsequently familiar characters: Captain Howard Largo and Old Man McGinnis. McGinnis is a major character in this novel, and his wonderful idiosyncracies are described with such ease and naturalness that he seems to have been sitting right before Hillerman as he wrote. And if we recall the author's youthful attention to the friendly one-upmanship of the good old boys who sat for hours spinning yarns on his father's porch, then McGinnis's provenance seems clear. At one point, Leaphorn asks the bourbon-sipping McGinnis whether Hosteen Tso had anything worth killing for.

McGinnis snorted. "There ain't nothing around here worth killing for," he said. "Put it all together and this whole Short Mountain country ain't worth hitting a man with a stick for."

"What do you think, then?" Leaphorn asked. "Anything that would help."

The old man communed with the inch of amber left in

the Coca-Cola glass. "I can tell you a story," he said finally. "If you don't mind having your time wasted."

"I'd like to hear it," Leaphorn said.

"Part of it's true," McGinnis said. "And some of it's probably Navajo bullshit." (82)

Now *there* is a writer who has listened to people speaking. And listened to old men speaking. You can almost hear the Oklahoma drawl in McGinnis's voice. But he isn't the only new character described in such convincing detail. The possessiveness of the beautiful and wilful Theodora Adams, whom both Leaphorn and McGinnis examine with the jaded eyes of men who are happy not to be involved with such a woman, is striking in its realism. And while female characters are never traced with the detail devoted to male characters in Hillerman's novels, both Listening Woman and Adams are superbly drawn nonetheless. As if perhaps to counterbalance the negative image of this somewhat destructive woman, Hillerman spends a long time describing a *Kinaalda*, or girl's puberty ceremony, attended by Leaphorn.

[Leaphorn] felt a fierce pride in his people, and in this celebration of womanhood. The Dinee had always respected the female equally with the male — giving her equality in property, in metaphysics and in clan — recognizing the mother's role in the footsteps of Changing Woman as the preserver of the Navajo Way. (94)

The book concludes with a final act of defiance on Leaphorn's part. He has recovered hundreds of thousands of dollars of stolen booty from a robbery, yet instead of bringing it with him, he leaves the money in a cave, the entrance of which is about to be blocked by a massive detonation of dynamite. Why? Because inside that cave he has discovered a holy Navajo site, which would be lost forever if the cave entrance were blocked. So he leaves the money inside, and waits.

Canyon Largo Navajo Rock Art, New Mexico.

At 4:02 the blackness at the cliff base became a blinding flash of white light. Seconds passed. A tremendous muffled thump echoed across the water, followed by a rumbling. Slabs of rocks falling inside the cave. Too many rocks for the white men to remove to clear the path to Standing Medicine's sand paintings, Leaphorn thought. But not too many rocks to remove to salvage a canvas bag heavy with cash. (199)

Thus does Leaphorn vanquish both the murderous intent of the kidnappers and the arrogant might of the white man. After the most physically arduous challenge of what would prove to be an astonishingly redoubtable career, after he has killed three self-described warriors of the Buffalo Society, Leaphorn succeeds in making their death a victory for all the Navajo people, by saving the sacred site.

10

By the time Tony Hillerman published *People of Darkness* (1980), his fourth Navajo mystery, he had begun to receive quite a bit of recognition in both the Navajo world and that of the Southwest literary establishment. Although his books were mysteries, their obvious literary merit had garnered Hillerman fans from virtually every stratum of society.

Hillerman's most important readers, however, remained those who were as deeply attached to the Navajo landscape as he was. This primarily included Navajos, yet it also meant Hopis, Zuñis, Apaches, and Pueblos. It meant old desert rats who had worked in the strip mines or oil fields decades earlier. It meant white teachers, traders, and other long-term residents. And it even meant Navajo tribal policemen. Thus many of Hillerman's readers, at least before he attained best-seller status, knew the landscape of the Big Reservation, and the customs of its inhabitants, far better than he. So when Tony Hillerman slipped up in his description of Chaco Wash, or in the telling of a part of the origin myth, there were always plenty of concerned readers present to let him know about his errors.

In a 1985 article in *Impact* magazine, published by the *Albuquerque Journal*, Della Toadlena, an English teacher at Navajo Community College in Tsalie, Arizona, took Hillerman to task for several errors which she felt were severe enough to warrant reprimand. She cites discrepancies in his descriptions of witchcraft, argues that it should have been an Evil Way ceremony rather than an Enemy Way ceremony in *The Blessing Way*, and that even the Enemy Way is wrongly described. She also tackles Hillerman's extensive description of the *Kinaalda*, or puberty rite, in *Listening Woman*, concluding that he has messed up several important elements.

Despite her harsh criticisms, Toadlena goes on to offer encouragement:

At first I didn't like Hillerman's discrepancies, but later I felt Hillerman might be purposely presenting the ceremonies erroneously in an attempt to protect the people. A medicine man will not give away all that he knows of a story or a legend, but will hold back a small portion or distort it in some small way to protect himself. If Hillerman's purpose is to retain the power of the ceremonies by confusing them, I appreciate the gesture. . . . My message to Tony Hillerman is: Keep those marvelous books coming because some Navajo children who would not ordinarily be interested in books are reading them. (7)

Tony Hillerman has never indicated that his aim is to protect the sanctity of the Navajo rituals by distorting facts. Though Jim Chee, like Della Toadlena, has remarked upon the tendency of most *hataali*, or medicine men, not least of all his uncle Frank Sam Nakai, to withhold secrets from disciples until they have earned the right to access them, Hillerman himself, as an author and ex-journalist, has always sought to be as accurate as possible.

I want my facts to be right, and I want people to respect their being right. I'm always checking up on myself too. When Navajos come to a book signing in Farmington or Gallup, I ask if they caught anything I'm wrong about. Once in a while they do, and when they tell me my mistake, I don't make it again. (Bernell and Karni 13)

Hillerman would likely counter Toadlena's arguments by saying that on the Big Reservation, the way certain ceremonies are performed varies as one moves from east to west across the enormous expanse of land. Yet while Hillerman has readily acknowledged certain minor errors of fact, his most blatant factual inaccuracy was the result of a deliberate choice, and he has regretted the decision ever since.

97

In *The Dark Wind* (1982), Hillerman moved the town of Burnt Water seventy-five miles north, simply because he liked the name. To the inhabitants of that region, this was akin to making Manhattan a mountain, or placing Los Angeles in British Columbia.

> The people who read my books . . . are the sort who can write you a letter that says, "Dear Mr. Hillerman, creosote brush does not grow at that altitude," or "Dear Mr. Hillerman, you will not find limestone deposits thick enough to be in this kind of cave in that part of the Navajo Reservation." When I had the gall to move Burnt Water, there was all kinds of consternation and confusion at Hubbell's Trading Post and other places of note. (qtd. in Ward 17)

People of Darkness introduced readers to a brand new set of characters, most notably Jim Chee. Chee evolved from a confluence of literary and legal forces. On one hand, Hillerman had been considering for some time the replacement of Leaphorn with a younger, more flexible character. Spurred on by the conflict regarding ownership of Leaphorn's character, he tried several versions before hitting on Jim Chee. Among these, interestingly enough, was a younger Joe Leaphorn, fresh-faced and only just beginning his career. There are precedents for such large-scale flashbacks. For example, in the series of adventure novels by C.S. Forester chronicling the naval career of Horatio Hornblower, Forester skipped from one rank to another without worrying about the consequences, portraying Hornblower the commodore in one book and following that with Hornblower the midshipman, or some such lowly rank. Yet Hillerman was uncomfortable with this device. Having already drawn Leaphorn's character with such depth and precision, fitting the younger man into the mould of his older self would have been far too constraining. And so, having discarded the possibility of a younger Leaphorn and a series of Lieutenant Begays, Hillerman brought Jim Chee — the college-educated tribal cop studying to be a shaman — to life.

Tony Hillerman's Navajo novels can be grouped in threes. The first three mysteries all feature Joe Leaphorn. The following three — *People of Darkness, The Dark Wind*, and *The Ghostway* — all feature Jim Chee. And the next three have Leaphorn and Chee working together. Of course, so do the next two, but the coherence of the first sets remains despite the later appearance of *Coyote Waits* and *Sacred Clowns*.

Of the three Jim Chee books, *The Ghostway* is the least typical of Hillerman's mysteries, and for that reason it may be the most intriguing, although all three of these novels are superb. In *The Ghostway*, Chee spends much of his time in Los Angeles, where his encounters with white police and Los Angeles citizens provoke constant amazement on the Navajo policeman's part. Of all the many interrogations to be found in Hillerman's novels, interrogations which often stand out as highlights of each book, none is so unusual, nor so compelling, as Jim Chee's questioning of Mr. Berger, the elderly stroke victim confined to a walker and a seniors home. Chee's conversation with the irascible yet tenacious Berger, through a chainlink fence dividing the seniors home from a motel parking lot, is filled with strained emotion, pathos, humour, and heart-stopping realism. It is worthy of Chee's visit to Los Angeles, the film-noir and hardboiled-cop capital of the world, that he should engage in such a thrilling dialogue with this perfectly infirm yet observant witness. And Chee too is a witness:

This was a side of white culture he'd never seen before. He'd read about it, but it had seemed too unreal to make an impression — this business of penning up the old. The fence was about six feet high, with the topmost foot tilted inward. Hard for an old woman to climb that, Chee thought. Impossible if she was tied in a wheelchair. Los Angeles seemed safe from these particular old people. (73)

Later, however, after Chee has grown fully disgusted with the ruthlessness of Los Angeles, with the abandoned elders and the child prostitutes, he makes a startling discovery, one that is eminently typical of Hillerman:

> The black man at the bus stop put his hand in his rear pocket and scratched his rump. Watching, Chee became aware that his own rump was itching. He scratched, and made himself aware of his hypocrisy.
>
> All alike under the skin, he thought, in every important way, despite my Navajo superiority. We want to eat, to sleep, to copulate and reproduce our genes, to be warm and dry and safe against tomorrow. Those are the important things, so what's my hang-up? (105)

Indeed, whenever Tony Hillerman has been questioned regarding his right to write about Navajo life, thoughts, and culture, he has responded with a similar argument: "What's your hang-up?" Hillerman likes to turn the tables by asking whether his critic is implying that we *are* all different under the skin, whether race is in fact a determining factor, whether the critic is himself endorsing racism. "I grew up with Indians," Hillerman has said, "and when you realize we are all alike, then there's no problem in writing about anyone" (qtd. in Harris 2). In a nutshell, this is Hillerman's guiding principle, and the foundation of his moral code: We are all alike. Not in the way we pray, or the way we talk, or the way we tie our shoes — these things vary from place to place and person to person, and thus we should recognize their relativity. But in essence, we are all the same under the skin, and this must be recognized as an absolute truth. Those who violate relative codes are to be laughed at, or admired for their individuality, or ignored perhaps. But those who violate the absolute principle of our common bond, who struggle to oppress others, or to denigrate them, or to exploit them — these individuals are to be condemned, and resisted. It comes down to a single word: respect.

This principle, which has won him great praise from some quarters, has also stirred up a great deal of resentment and anger in others. Interestingly, both the most meaningful praise and the most vitriolic attacks have come from the native people he has written about.

The attacks have been from Hopi critics, who condemned Hillerman's "exploitation" of their religion in *The Dark Wind*. The book centres on a drug-smuggling operation on the Checkerboard Reservation, one which reaches its climax during a Hopi religious ritual. Hopi religion, as Hillerman emphasizes in *The Dark Wind*, is an extremely secretive set of practices and beliefs. Although Hillerman had gained all of his information from anthropology books available to anyone interested in reading them, he was condemned for having plundered the Hopi cultural heritage.

However, Hillerman was not the only person to come under fire. The rights to his book were bought by Robert Redford's Wildwood Films, along with the rights to *Skinwalkers* and *A Thief of Time*, and in 1990 it was made into a feature film starring Lou Diamond Phillips as Jim Chee. When Redford's company set out to film *The Dark Wind*, they were refused permission to shoot on Hopi land, and to use the names of Hopi towns in the film. Attempts to portray Hopi religious rites aroused ferocious opposition and indignation from the Hopi people. Redford had declared his intention to cooperate in every way possible with the Hopi, and so the producers substantially altered all of the scenes involving religion. The result was satisfactory to no one, however, and to date *The Dark Wind* has not been released commercially. Despite the problems associated with the film, Redford expressed a great deal of respect for Hillerman, saying,

> He is very unfettered by either success or too much trouble around him. . . . He travels his own route and at his own pace. He's rare in that he has that wonderful sense of structure of storytelling and a very clear eye as to the real nature of the Navajo. (qtd. in Benke D1)

While the Hopi response underscores the sensitivity of certain cultures to outside interference, as well as how good intentions can lead to situations where individuals and tribes feel legitimately misrepresented and exploited, the Navajo response to Hillerman's books has been far more encouraging. In fact, one of Hillerman's proudest possessions is an award he was given by the Navajo nation. At the Window Rock Tribal Fair in 1987, he was named a "Special Friend of the Dineh" for "authentically portraying the strength and dignity of traditional Navajo culture" ("Hillerman, Tony" 261). Hillerman was also made Grand Marshal of the parade that year, although when he was asked to ride a horse, he replied that he'd do so only if the horse was as old as he was. The Navajos provided a convertible instead.

Hillerman's public recognition validated all of the time he had spent tracking down details of Navajo culture, religion, and values. If confirmed that his work was seen as essentially sympathetic to the Navajo way of life, and worthy of respect and commendation. And yet, Hillerman was not always so certain that his role was a valuable one.

At first I was embarrassed that my books were read in Navajo schools. I considered it an enormous responsibility and an honour which I hadn't really earned. After all, I was a white man myself. But one day a Navajo librarian told me that she was proud to be a Navajo after reading my books, that for once Indians were really heroes and always won, even if it was only in a detective novel. (Geffard; my translation)

Hillerman's fan mail increased steadily, and a great deal of it came from Navajos. Once he even received a letter from a white woman in Los Angeles who had married a Navajo named Begay. She wrote to tell Hillerman that after reading his books, and in particular the part about Begays, she had reached a much better understanding of her husband!

How has Tony Hillerman managed to grasp so thoroughly the Navajo culture? He believes that it has more to do with class, and with rural values, than it does with anything else.

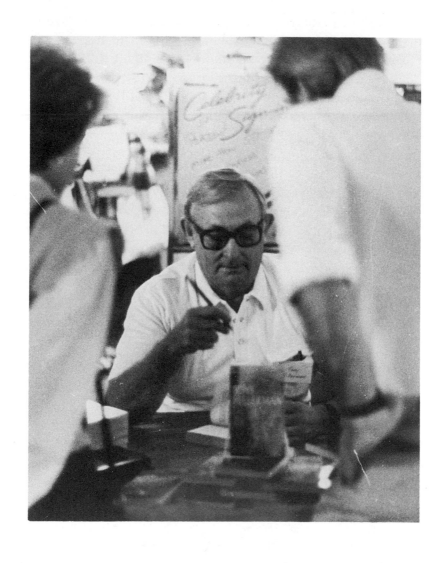

PHOTO COURTESY CENTER FOR SOUTHWEST RESEARCH
NO. 000-501-0005

You don't walk right up to a Navajo's yard and pound on his door. You didn't do that in Pott County either. You stopped out at the gate. The house was built up there on a hill and there was a gate and you stopped down there and screwed around a little, let the dogs bark, let the people get their overalls buttoned up, and *then* you drove on up. One reason I think I relate to Navajos is that I have much more in common as a farmer from Pottawatomie County, Okla., with the Navajos than I do with most of the faculty members from the University of New Mexico who grew up knowing they were going to college, a good college, and then grad school. (qtd. in Carr 9)

On June 30, 1985, Tony Hillerman finally said goodbye to those colleagues at the University of New Mexico. He had taught at UNM for almost twenty-two years, and served as chair of his department for eight of those. He had twice been a special assistant to the president, and during his entire tenure he had taken only two sabbaticals. At about this time he also experienced another significant rearrangement of his professional career: Joan Kahn, who had edited every novel he had written, left Harper and Row and moved to St. Martin's Press. She was replaced by Larry Ashmead. Hillerman had liked working with Kahn. According to Hillerman, she "wanted the books to be right and not drag. She didn't care whether anybody bought them or not. I learned a lot from her. About the time I had it pretty well down, she went to another publisher" (qtd. in Campbell A30). Although Hillerman has enjoyed working with Ashmead, his new editor has a somewhat different orientation. Ashmead saw in Hillerman's work the potential for significantly higher sales figures, and since Ashmead's arrival Hillerman's books have been consistently making their way onto best-seller lists. Although this has been a positive development for Harper and Row, for Tony Hillerman, the good old boy from Oklahoma, success has proven, in a small way, to be a burden.

II

Leaphorn and Chee, each in their way, are loners, outsiders, they never really cooperate with the FBI even though they are supposed to. They sort of look on the white man's law, which they're supposed to be enforcing, as all very well, as long as it makes sense to them. And as long as it doesn't violate the much higher way of life, which is the Navajo way of life. (*Writing the Southwest*)

Loners and outsiders. Leaphorn and Chee. A policeman and a shaman/policeman. Each in his own way standing outside the group, outside the community. Yet each in his own way contributing to the fundamental balance and well-being of his community, his nation, his people. And the creator of these two all-too-human heroes, these insecure, troubled, ever-victorious personae, is constantly reflected in their thoughts and actions. In Joe Leaphorn, Tony Hillerman gives voice to the quick-witted yet jaded observer, the man who does his duty because he likes doing it, yet who is never genuinely comfortable with the responsibility and knowledge that duty confers upon him. In Jim Chee, Hillerman emphasizes the more spiritual side of his own pious character, the youthful idealist whose faith is uncertain yet whose passion is absolute. It was inevitable, and, from a reader's perspective, entirely desirable, that these two complex individuals should meet. In Hillerman's seventh Navajo mystery, *Skinwalkers* (1986), they do.

Beyond the poetic justice (no pun intended) of their encounter, and the commercial potential of their meeting for Harper and Row, Hillerman had a practical, authorial reason for uniting his two protagonists.

Navajo police on patrol, south-west of Tuba City.

PHOTO COURTESY TERRENCE MOORE

[Leaphorn] was too old; he was too sophisticated; he'd been to FBI academy; he knew the ways of the white man, and they didn't intrigue him, particularly. So by the time I was writing the third book, *Listening Woman*, I was thinking this guy's not what I need. . . . Chee would be what Navajo kids would call a "john," a hillbilly Navajo, a red-neck country bumpkin who would come into school and would speak good Navajo but not very good English. The city boy Navajos would look on him with scorn and contempt. That wouldn't be true of Leaphorn. Different personalities, I hope, but then I said, "am I just kidding myself? Did I just change him in superficial ways or do I have a new character?" I thought I did, but I decided to put them together in *Skinwalkers*. Then I think I proved it, to myself at least. Now I'm satisfied I've got two different men. (Ross and Silet 120–21)

Interestingly, and satisfyingly, Chee and Leaphorn don't really like each other at first. Leaphorn suspects that Chee is dishonest because an assailant is trying to kill him, and both Leaphorn and Largo agree that any officer who causes someone to stalk him has probably done something illegal to deserve it. But eventually Leaphorn gains a grudging respect for Chee's intelligence and observational skills. Chee, on the other hand, respects Leaphorn because of his reputation and seniority, yet finds the actual man somewhat arrogant and hard to deal with. Nor do they work well together, because each is unorthodox and intuitive, holding back incomplete ideas and potential leads until they have been more fully developed. Interestingly, despite Chee's more explicit spirituality, it is Leaphorn who more consistently admires the landscapes, stopping regularly to ponder and stare at the land. Jim Chee too loves his environment, but he is more introspective than Leaphorn, and pauses less often in this manner. This aestheticism, so unlike the city-dweller's casual disregard for his or her surroundings, is something that Hillerman admires in the Navajo, though in this he cannot claim a kinship based upon his rural upbringing.

Growing up around rednecks, hell, being one myself, I didn't know very many people who ever talked about natural beauty. . . . They seemed really unconscious of it. But I find it remarkable how many Navajos will talk frankly and almost emotionally about the beauty around them. (qtd. in Ward 21–23)

This appreciation of nature is but one aspect of Hillerman's fondness of and respect for Navajo culture and values. His respect manifests itself not just in Jim Chee and Joe Leaphorn, but in the many minor characters who appear in Hillerman's novels.

I like [the Navajo] emphasis on taking care of the family. . . . I like the dignity they give their women. I like their attitude about material possessions. They just don't attach any importance to them. There's the idea that if you own too much, you probably aren't taking care of your family.

I like the emphasis they have on beauty, aesthetics — so many Navajos seem to have a good eye for the sunset, the pleasing design.

I like their sense of humor, their stoic endurance of whatever comes down. They endure. (qtd. in Benke D10)

I think it shows an illuminated intelligence not to simply let your reason take you to the limits of the rational and say, since I can't understand beyond this point, it doesn't exist. Navajos get into this poetry that tries to connect the knowable with the unknowable and accepts the unknowing. (qtd. in Gaugenmaier 56–57)

As had become clear during the years leading up to the publication of *Skinwalkers*, Hillerman was not the only one impressed by these values. The respect shown by Hillerman for Navajo culture was certainly an essential reason for the growing popularity of his books. Hillerman's fan mail included a remarkable cross-section of correspondents: from budding journalists and novelists to budding critics suggesting all kinds of minor and major changes; from firearms experts pointing out that a certain gun would be more appropriate for a certain killing than the one Hillerman had described, to a community of monks writing to thank him for his fine writing; from an ex-CIA agent to the editor of *Soldier of Fortune* magazine; from people blaming Hillerman for a decline in the quality of their work because they couldn't resist reading his novels on the job, to a worker in the Bulgarian Writer's Union wanting an interview for *Literaturen Front*, the association's official organ; from a fingerprinting expert to people asking for travel advice for their upcoming trip to the Southwest!

Perhaps more remarkable than the enormous volume of fan mail Hillerman's books generated is the fact that for many years (until the volume simply became too large) Tony Hillerman answered almost every letter himself. And on top of this deluge of correspondence, Hillerman's home telephone rang constantly. It remained stubbornly listed in the Albuquerque phone book until 1990, when one caller, the twenty-third of that particular morning, pushed Tony and Marie Hillerman over the brink. A man telephoned long-distance from somewhere in the Midwest to make an inquiry: he was planning a road trip to the Four Corners region, and he had read that Hillerman drove an Isuzu Trooper, and so did he, and he was wondering whether Hillerman would be able to recommend a good garage for him just in case he had car trouble during his vacation. Hillerman politely excused himself and immediately requested an unlisted phone number.

The reason such calls were coming in was that Hillerman was no longer just a genre writer, no longer only a local celebrity. With the publication of *Skinwalkers*, and subsequent Leaphorn-Chee collaborations, Hillerman had become one of the most widely read mystery writers in America. Harper and Row's initial print run for *The Ghostway*, when it was released in the fall of 1984, was 10,000 copies. By the following May over 17,000 hardcover copies had been shipped. These were certainly respectable numbers, but far from best-seller status. For *Skinwalkers*, Harper and Row upped the promotional budget from $10,000 to $40,000, and the first hardcover printing to 50,000. The book was released on November 5, 1986, well in advance of its official publication date of January 1, 1987, and by January 1988 there were over 100,000 copies in print, making *Skinwalkers* the first Hillerman to reach the best-seller list. *Skinwalkers* won the Anthony Award from the Boucheron (the most important convention of mystery writers, publishers, and fans), the Grand Prix de Littérature Policier in France, for best foreign crime novel, and the Golden Spur Award of the Western Writers of America for Best Novel of the Year. Suddenly, Hillerman was a celebrity.

But his success didn't stop there. Hillerman's next book, *A Thief of Time*, was the second of a two-book contract with Harper and Row, and for this one the publisher pulled out all the stops. *A Thief of Time*'s first printing was 75,000 copies. The book was released in the spring of 1988, and by June there were 90,000 copies in print. By mid-August, 100,000. And by September 21, mere months after the book was released, there were 145,000 hardcover copies of *A Thief of Time* in print. This second Leaphorn-Chee collaboration, like *Skinwalkers* before it, won the French prize for best foreign mystery.

Part of Hillerman's responsibilities to Harper and Row included travelling to various locales to promote his books. For *Skinwalkers*, Hillerman travelled throughout January 1987 to Santa Fe, Tucson, Flagstaff, Phoenix, Los Angeles, San Diego, San Francisco, Denver, Salt Lake City, Washington, Boston, and New York. The latter stages were undertaken in the midst of a fierce midwinter storm, but Hillerman found his adventure exciting despite the discomfort. Just over a year later, Hillerman again took off on a book tour, this one even more ambitious than the last. Over the course of five weeks, he visited all of the cities he had been to for *Skinwalkers*, as well as Chicago and Seattle.

While in Washington during the latter tour, Hillerman visited the Smithsonian to investigate a story idea he had been developing. It had to do with the then-prominent movement to have the bones of many thousands of native Americans, currently housed in the Smithsonian's vast archives as "specimens yet to be examined," returned to their descendants for reinterment in their natural resting ground. This story idea would become the basis of *Talking God* (1989), the third Chee-Leaphorn novel.

From a critical perspective, despite *Talking God* being by far the most commercially successful Hillerman novel up to that time, it might be argued that it was also the point at which Hillerman's enthusiasm for his characters and their mysteries began to wane. The book certainly had its moments, and it is only slightly less engaging than *A Thief of Time*, yet it seems to lack something of the intensity, the urgency, which characterized Hillerman's earlier novels. Hillerman was forced to carry the baggage of all his earlier novels every time he set out to write a new book, and as this baggage grew, it became harder and harder to write fresh, creative novels unaffected by the stake which thousands of readers now had in his work. *Talking God* was the ninth Navajo mystery in the series, and what with his constant travelling, his speaking engagements, and the endless requests for interviews, Tony Hillerman was beginning to feel the need to slow down. By the time *Talking God* was published, he had reached the age of sixty-four. He needed a rest.

12

In 1989 Tony Hillerman was offered a new contract by Harper and Row, who wanted two more novels. Was he still interested in writing about Jim Chee and Joe Leaphorn? Possibly. But he wanted to do others things too. Like move. The Hillermans had lived for over twenty-five years in the same house, the one they had bought when they moved to Albuquerque from Santa Fe in 1963. But they had since then acquired a parcel of land by the Rio Grande, in a neighbourhood which was far more posh. Despite his natural suspicion of any such ritzy environment, Tony finally thought it was time to get away. There was virtually no privacy anymore, and since they had enough money now, they may as well move into a home that offered them a few extras. The Hillermans built themselves a lovely adobe home and moved into it.

Hillerman signed the contract for two more books, but these would certainly be the last two. After all, there were other things to write about! Those two books have now been published, and it seems unlikely, based upon a reading of *Sacred Clowns* (1993), that there will be any more Navajo mysteries. For *Sacred Clowns* seems to be clearly intended as an epilogue to the series. In it we find Joe Leaphorn finally settling down with Louisa Bourebon-ette, and Jim Chee finally making promising headway with Janet Pete. Neither *Sacred Clowns* nor *Coyote Waits* is up to the quality of the earlier novels, yet owing to the ever-growing interest in Hillerman's work, they have been the most successful by far in terms of sales. Harper and Row printed a truly astounding number of hardcover copies of *Sacred Clowns*: 400,000. And that was only the first edition!

Yet, if Hillerman's enthusiasm and inventiveness in the realm of Navajo mysteries seems to have waned somewhat, there is

Tony in the February 10, 1991, issue of The Daily Oklahoman.

good reason for this lapse. In 1991 Hillerman was diagnosed with prostate cancer and underwent surgery on three separate occasions. He also found that his arthritis had gotten so bad that it made typing impossible. And finally, on October 7, 1991, Barney Hillerman died unexpectedly.

The two brothers had collaborated on a book called *Hillerman Country* which had been released just one week earlier. *Hillerman Country* is a wonderful book combining Barney's beautiful photographs of New Mexico, Arizona, and Utah with rambling essays on the region by Tony. Barney spent his entire life working as a freelance photographer in Oklahoma, and while he and Tony were very different, his death was nonetheless an enormous tragedy for Tony. In an article devoted to remembering his brother, Tony described Barney as the "most Christian person I've ever known" (qtd. in Mercer 42).

Tony Hillerman's family life has always centred on his wife Marie. It was she who encouraged Tony to try the things he doubted he would be able to accomplish — to go back to school, to try writing fiction. In one of the only interviews he has given in which he has spoken of his private life, Tony Hillerman had this to say about Marie:

My wife is a wonderful lady, and we've been married almost, let's see, we were married in 1948. Forty years almost, isn't it? Okay, now she was Phi Beta Kappa, I was a gentlemanly C. She is the brains of the family. She is the woman who speaks Spanish, French, Swedish and German as well as English. She's the one who is always up on, you know, . . . if it's been reviewed in the *New York Times Book Review*, Marie's read it. My wife and I are best of friends, and neither one of us thinks we're living with a successful writer. We both think it's some kind of weird thing, but she's tremendously supportive. She thinks I do too much of this running around because it wears me out. She's protective of me. . . .

She likes me for some reason that I don't know, but it doesn't have anything to do with writing, but she does read my stuff . . . and if she says Tony that's good, I think well I better go back and work on it some more. If she said that's great, then I think it's about right. She knows how to criticize my work to tell me what she thinks of it without hurting my feelings. . . .

She goes with me frequently when I go to the reservation and is my botanical flora and fauna authority, geology authority and stuff like that. I'd say Marie, what kind of grass is that over there near Chaco Canyon, she'd say well it's some Gramma grass and some Cheat grass. So I don't make as many mistakes as I would otherwise. (Ross and Silet 134–35)

Two of Tony and Marie's six children, Anne and Janet, have followed to some extent in their father's footsteps. Anne is currently a reporter for the *Albuquerque Tribune* and has written two children's books, while Janet illustrated her father's children's story, *The Boy Who Made Dragonfly*. Tony and Marie have eight grandchildren.

What does the future hold for Tony Hillerman? In keeping with his lifelong desire to try new things, he has embarked upon the writing of his first non-Navajo novel since *The Fly on the Wall*, written more than twenty years ago. This new novel will be set in Asia, and will focus upon the situation of a young man caught up unexpectedly in the turmoil of Southeast Asian politics and war. It will also explore the beliefs and doctrines of an obscure Cambodian Buddhist sect, whose history Hillerman has been studiously reading up on for some time. Having recovered from the physical and emotional traumas which contributed to the three-year gap between *Coyote Waits* and *Sacred Clowns*, as well as feeling free of the pressure of producing yet another Navajo novel, Hillerman is once again excited by the challenge of writing. The urge to try writing a different kind of book has been growing in Hillerman for some time. In 1985 he went to Manila to research the story he is currently writing, which concerns the search by a man for his late brother's illegitimate daughter. "This one is going to be hard to write," Hillerman said in a recent interview. "Not because it's Asian, but because the chief character is so complex. I've wanted to write it for a long time but I didn't think I was good enough before" (Reed C3).

This humility has been an essential thread through Tony Hillerman's life. Despite his almost endless string of successes, he has never ceased questioning himself. To this day he questions his abilities as a writer. As an editor and professor he questioned his own ethics, his own accomplishments, and he did so more or less publicly. Or, perhaps it is more accurate to say that he found an outlet for those doubts. Instead of turning them inward and letting them cripple him, he has always had the courage to turn those doubts into a story of some kind and let it out. His constancy in this regard is indicative of Hillerman's own true faith in the honesty and goodwill of the people who surround him — his family, his friends, his neighbours, and his community. It is that faith in community, the belief that if he gave of himself he would never truly be endangered, which has guided his movements from that early heroic encounter with bullets, to the many later challenges he met as the editor of a major newspaper and the chair of a university department, to say nothing of his audacity in writing about the Navajo. Virtue, civic virtue, devotion to his fellow human — these are also outgrowths of Hillerman's essentially pious nature. Tony Hillerman is a practising Catholic and says grace before every meal, yet he is also quite evidently a man who respects all religions, all spiritual beliefs. Hillerman has consistently demonstrated that humility, imagination, respect, and love still have a place in the public life. Indeed, he has consistently and seemingly single-handedly affirmed that there *is* such a thing as a public life: that honesty, courage, creativity, and compassion are simultaneously the keys to fulfilment of the individual and the keys to the health of the community. Many of the citizens of Albuquerque consider Tony Hillerman to be their unofficial mayor. His commitment to his community has given him that recognition, the recognition afforded an individual who has lived, to the benefit of many others, a public life. There are few more worthy honours.

APPENDIX

In 1973 the graduating students of Zuni High School voted to invite Tony Hillerman as their commencement speaker. Following is the text of Hillerman's speech:

Tonight these high school seniors and I have something in common . . . They have never graduated from high school before . . . and I've never before delivered a commencement speech . . . In a few minutes, we'll all have that behind us.

When I was told that your graduating class had decided to ask me to deliver this speech I was greatly honored. I was also surprised. I asked myself why I was picked. And the only answer I could think of was because I have written books about Zuni.

Then I asked myself what I could think of to say that would be of any possible use to you at this important turning point in your lives. Once again I thought of one of these books. Behind it there's a story which I think might interest you.

Nobody knows exactly when this story was first told. Ethnologists and anthropologists — the people who study such things — suspect it began 500 or 600 years ago. They know it was told before your people moved to the present site of Zuni village — when they were living south of here at a site which was abandoned centuries ago.

The story tells about a time when the people of Zuni were very rich. Year after year the rains fell and great crops grew and all the store rooms of the village were overflowing. The leaders of the village decided that instead of building more store rooms, or sharing their great wealth with their neighbors, they would hold a sort of public spectacle. They would divide into teams, spend days cooking bread, boiling mush and making other foods.

And then they would invite the Navajos, and the Hopis, and the Acomas and Lagunas and Apaches to come and watch. Then they would have a great War Game in which food would be used as weapons. They would throw it at one another. And, by wasting it in this fashion, they demonstrated to all their neighbors just how rich they were.

To make a long and intricate story shorter, I'll simply say that in addition to this wastefulness, the people were doing some other things wrong. They were being unfriendly to strangers, and unkind to those in their own village who needed help.

In punishment for this sort of conduct the Corn Maidens stop the rain. There's a great drought, and a famine and the people are finally forced to evacuate their village and live with the Hopis to keep from starving. And they accidentally leave behind two children and an old woman.

As I said, it's a long and complicated story in their adventures — and like such stories it is used to teach the real values of life. It teaches friendship, and loyalty, and hospitality, and love are things that are really important — and pride, and anger, and selfishness and wastefulness bear within themselves their own punishment.

Since I was old enough to remember, I have loved stories, and sort of collected them. And I can tell you that you won't find one any better than this Zuni story. I'm sure many of you here know that old story much better than I do. And what I really want to tell you about is a story behind the story.

Almost a hundred years ago, in 1879 — a man named Frank Hamilton Cushing was sent here by the American Ethnological Society. He was supposed to study the Zuni language and Zuni customs. Your great-great grandparents gave Mr. Cushing a home to live in, and food, and began teaching him how to speak Zuni and all about the history of the people. Among other things, your great-great grandparents taught Mr. Cushing the story I've just been telling you about. Cushing was impressed by it. He wrote it down and decided he would get it published so other white men would know more about the Zuni people.

Zuni-Shalako.

But he ran into a problem. He found out that white men weren't interested in the Zuni people. He couldn't get anyone to publish the story. Finally, he stuck it into an article on baking bread and got it published in a paper put out by a company that manufactured flour.

Ninety years passed. I heard the story. Like Cushing I was impressed by it. I wrote it down. I sent it off to a publisher. Here things started going very differently for me than they did for Cushing. As soon as they saw it, the editors of one of America's biggest publishing houses wanted to print it. They published it. It was written about by the book reviewers all over the country. A Library Association chose it for an award. And today you can find it in libraries all over the country.

The point I want to make is simply this.

The story hasn't changed. It has been told the same way for hundreds of years and as Cushing and I wrote it down, it was pretty much the same. It still teaches the same values that it taught in 1879, and 1779, and 1679, and on way back before the first white man came to this country.

The story hasn't changed. What has changed is the world outside Zuni.

When Cushing was trying to get that Zuni story published, the white man didn't want to know about your people. The white man thought he had all the answers. He was sure his way was the right way. He didn't think he had anything to learn from an old Zuni lesson.

A lot of things have happened since then. The world outside Zuni has seen millions of people killed in a series of its white man's wars. He's seen the hydrogen bomb and the missiles developed so that when he gets into another war he'll be killing billions instead of millions. He's seen the country start running out of such things as natural gas and oil — proving that you can't keep wasting everything forever without being punished for it. He's seen that getting richer doesn't seem to make him any happier. He's seen enough to know that there's something wrong with some of the white man's ways. He's learned enough to know that he's got something to learn from a society like your own — because he's just beginning to become conscious of what your people have done that his people haven't been able to manage. What's that? —

Well, for example —

Your people have lived here for about 40 or 50 generations without ever starting a single war with your neighbours.

And, without being warlike, your people have always managed to defend themselves whenever they were attacked.

And, as far back as written history goes, and beyond that into oral history, your people have always been famous for hospitality, and friendship, and sharing the bounty of the earth with those who need it.

And, your people have lived here for 400 years without ruining the land you live on — or polluting the air, or dirtying the water. The white man's way all too often ruins the land in single generation.

And now — at last — we come to the point of all this.

As high school graduates many of you will be leaving Zuni soon — either to continue your education or to look for opportunity in employment.

I urge you, if you leave the Zuni Reservation, not to leave the ways of Zuni behind you. You will take with you what you have learned at this school from your teachers here. I hope you will also take you with you — and use — what your families have taught you about what is *really valuable* in this life.

The people outside of Zuni are only now beginning to learn that you have something very special here: an attitude about life, and nature, which is special and valuable. It would be very bad if you lost that value.

This Frank Hamilton Cushing I mentioned — the man who first wrote down the story which I call "The Boy Who Made the Dragonfly" — became convinced as he lived among your great-great grandparents that for him the Zuni Way was best. He asked to be allowed to become a Zuni. And your great-great grandparents initiated him into the Macaw Clan. And before he died he had become a member of the Bow Society and was very proud to be a Zuni.

I would be very proud to be a Zuni. I know that you must be too. And I hope that never changes.

CHRONOLOGY

1925	Tony Hillerman born 27 May in Sacred Heart, Oklahoma.
1930–38	Attends St. Mary's Academy.
1939–42	Attends Konawa High School.
1941	Gus Hillerman, Tony's father, dies 25 December.
1942	Enrolls at Oklahoma State University.
1943	Quits OSU to manage farm. Turns 18 and joins U.S. Army.
1944	Lands in France on D-Day.
1945	Defends mortar position and receives Silver Star. Wounded by grenade while on patrol in Alsace. Returns to U.S. for convalescent furlough in Oklahoma. Drives truck to Navajo Reserve.
1945–48	Attends University of Oklahoma.
1948	Marries Marie Elizabeth Unzner 16 August.
1948–49	Writer for *News Herald* in Borger, Texas.
1949–50	News editor for *Morning Press* in Lawton, Oklahoma.
1950–52	Reporter for United Press International in Oklahoma City.
1952–54	Santa Fe bureau chief for UPI.
1954–62	Reporter and editor at Santa Fe *New Mexican*.
1963	Attends University of New Mexico. Hired as assistant to UNM president Tom Popejoy. Buys house in Albuquerque.
1964	Hired as associate professor in journalism at UNM.
1966	Becomes chair of UNM Journalism Department.
1970	*The Blessing Way.*
1971	*The Fly on the Wall.*
1973	*The Great Taos Bank Robbery* and *Dance Hall of the Dead.*

Wins Edgar Allan Poe Award for Best Mystery Novel.
1974   Resigns chairmanship of Journalism Department. *New Mexico*, with photographer David Muench.
1975   *Rio Grande*, with photographer Robert Reynolds.
1976   Hired as assistant to UNM president William Davis. Awarded 1975 Dan Burrows Memorial Award for journalism.
1978   *Listening Woman.*
1980   *People of Darkness.*
1981   Leaves position as assistant to UNM president.
1982   *The Dark Wind.*
1984   *The Ghostway.*
1985   Retires from UNM Journalism Department 30 June.
1986   *Skinwalkers.*
1988   *A Thief of Time.*
1989   *Talking God.*
1990   *Coyote Waits.*
1991   *Hillerman Country.* Barney Hillerman, Tony's brother, dies 7 October.
1993   *Sacred Clowns.*

WORKS CONSULTED

Benke, Richard. "Filming Starts This Summer on Hillerman's 'Dark Wind.' " *Albuquerque Journal* 16 Feb. 1990: D1, D10.

Bernell, Sue, and Michaela Karni. Interview with Tony Hillerman, ts. Tony Hillerman Collection. Center for Southwest Research, U of New Mexico, Albuquerque. N.d.

Black, Charlotte. "Author's 'Roots' Nurture Career." *Albuquerque Tribune* 25 June 1982: B1.

Breslin, Catherine. "PW Interviews: Tony Hillerman." *Publishers Weekly* 10 June 1988: 57–58.

Campbell, Mary. "Author Uses Navajo Lore in Mysteries." *Los Angeles Times* 27 Oct. 1991: A30–A31.

Carr, John. "Tony Hillerman: Evil and a Good Ol' Boy." *Impact* [*Albuquerque Journal*] 5 Feb. 1985: 4–9.

Gaugenmaier, Judith Tabor. "The Mysteries of Tony Hillerman." *American West* Dec. 1989: 46–47, 56–58.

Geffard, François. "Rencontre avec Tony Hillerman." Interview. *L'Oeil de la lettre* [Paris] 1990.

Gorney, Cynthia. "Hillerman and His Navajo Mysteries: A Popular Author's Drive for Authenticity." *Washington Post* 29 Jan. 1987: C1–C2.

Harris, Jim. "Tony Hillerman's *Dance Hall of the Dead*." *The Greater Llano Estecado Southwest Heritage* 6.2 (1976): 2–6, 52.

Hieb, Louis A. *Tony Hillerman: A Bibliography, from The Blessing Way to Talking God*. Tucson: Press of the Gigantic Hound, 1990.

Hillerman, Tony. *The Blessing Way*. 1970. New York: Harper, 1990.

———. *Coyote Waits*. New York: Harper, 1990.

———. *Dance Hall of the Dead*. New York: Harper, 1973.

———. *The Dark Wind*. New York: Harper, 1982.

———. *The Fly on the Wall*. New York: Harper, 1971.

———. *The Ghostway*. 1984. New York: Harper, 1985.

———. *The Great Taos Bank Robbery, and Other Indian Country Affairs.*

Albuquerque: U of New Mexico Press, 1973.

———. Letter to Joan Kahn. 20 Sept. 1977. Tony Hillerman Collection. Center for Southwest Research, U of New Mexico, Albuquerque.

———. Letter to Mary McGinn. 28 July 1969. Tony Hillerman Collection. Center for Southwest Research, U of New Mexico, Albuquerque.

———. Letter to Mary McGinn. 1 Aug. 1969. Tony Hillerman Collection. Center for Southwest Research, U of New Mexico, Albuquerque.

———. *Listening Woman*. New York: Harper, 1978.

———. Notebook. Tony Hillerman Collection. Center for Southwest Research, U of New Mexico, Albuquerque.

———. *People of Darkness*. New York: Harper, 1980.

———. *Sacred Clowns*. New York: HarperCollins, 1993.

———. *Skinwalkers*. New York: Harper, 1986.

———. *Talking God*. New York: Harper, 1989.

———. *A Thief of Time*. New York: Harper, 1988.

———. "Tony Hillerman Remembers Sacred Heart." *Sacred Heart Newsletter* spring/summer 1993: 4. (Rpt. from *Oklahoma Today*.)

———. *Writing the Southwest*. Interview. KUNM, Albuquerque. 1988.

Hillerman, Tony, and Ernie Bulow. *Talking Mysteries: A Conversation with Tony Hillerman*. Albuquerque: U of New Mexico P, 1991.

Hillerman, Tony, and Barney Hillerman. *Hillerman Country: A Journey through the Southwest with Tony Hillerman*. New York: Harper-Collins, 1991.

"Hillerman, Tony." *Current Biography Yearbook 1992*. New York: Wilson, 1992. 258–61.

"Hillerman Winner of Press Award." *Albuquerque Journal* 15 Jan. 1976: C4.

Holt, Cynthia. "PW Interviews: Tony Hillerman." *Publishers Weekly* 24 Oct. 1980: 6–7.

Mercer, Robert. "The Brothers Hillerman: Barney and Tony Together." *Oklahoma Today* Jan.–Feb. 1992: 40–44.

Parfit, Michael. "Weaving Mysteries That Tell of Life among the Navajos." *Smithsonian* Dec. 1990: 92–105.

Reed, Ollie, Jr. "Here's to Your Health, Tony." *Albuquerque Tribune* 7 Sept. 1993: C1, C3.

Reid, Dixie. "Keeping Secrets." *Sacramento Bee* 28 May 1992: F1.

Ross, Dale H., and Charles L. P. Silet. "Interview with Tony Hiller-man." *Clues* [U of Iowa] fall/winter 1989: 121–35.

Sandstrom, Eve. "Making Crime Pay." *Sooner Magazine* 10.2 (1990): 3–10.

Smith, Lisa. "Redneck Populist: Native Oklahoman Hillerman Prefers Down-Home Approach to Writing Life." *Oklahoma Gazette* 12 Mar. 1992: 23.

Sooner Yearbook. Norman: U of Oklahoma, 1948.

Stahl, Beatrice. "He Stood Fearlessly." *Daily Oklahoman* 24 Apr. 1945: 12.

Toadlena, Della. "And Now a Few Words from the Other Side." *Impact* [*Albuquerque Journal*] 5 Feb. 1985: 6–7.

Ward, Alex. "Navajo Cops on the Case: Tony Hillerman Brings the Navajo Way to the World." *Albuquerque Monthly* Dec. 1989: 16–23.